THE Ornamental Edible Garden

DIANA ANTHONY
PHOTOGRAPHS by GIL HANLY

University of Hawai'i Press
Honolulu

For my grandsons Flynn and Charlie — may you always have picking baskets too!

Published in North America by
University of Hawai'i Press
2840 Kolowalu Street
Honolulu, HI 96822
www.uhpress.hawaii.edu

First published in New Zealand by
David Bateman Ltd
30 Tarndale Grove, Albany
Auckland 0745
New Zealand

Library of Congress Cataloging-in-Publication Data

Anthony, Diana.
  The ornamental edible garden / Diana Anthony ; photographs by Gil Hanly.
    p. cm.
  ISBN 978-0-8248-3672-6 (pbk. : alk. paper)
  1. Edible landscaping. 2. Organic gardening. 3. Vegetable gardening. I. Hanly, Gil. II. Title.
  SB475.9.E35A58 2012
  635.987--dc23
                    2011039857

Book design: Alice Bell
Photographs: Diana Anthony 104, 129 (top & bottom); iStock 60, 62, 63 (top), 64, 72
    (bottom), 73 (top), 85, 89; Maria Rodgers 134 (top); Shutterstock 55 (top & bottom), 66, 68
    (bottom), 75, 78 (top), 79, 90, 91 (top & bottom)
Garden plans & illustrations: Diana Anthony
Printed in China through Colorcraft Ltd, Hong Kong

Contents

Introduction

The concept & history of the edible garden

Gardens are always evocative. My passion for edible gardening was nurtured in childhood when a well-stocked plot of vegetables was as important to my family as fresh air and sunlight. Firm believers in the old adage 'one for the birds, one for the bugs, and one for me', all produce was grown in good home-made compost without recourse to toxic sprays or chemical fertilisers. I can still smell the rich chocolate earth and taste succulent young peas, scarlet sun-warmed tomatoes and soft fruits picked and eaten straight from the plant. I remember the magic (still undiminished half a century later!) of excavating the soil and finding tiny new golden-skinned potatoes.

A particular joy was to accompany my grandparents into their vegetable garden, carrying in my small hands their huge 'picking basket'. I was allowed to choose and harvest whichever edibles took my fancy, the rule being that I ate everything I picked — I can think of no better way of getting a small child to eat greens!

Highly productive though these gardens were, the growing of food was strictly a utilitarian process, all vegetables marching in rigid ranks and rows, straight as soldiers, across a plot discreetly tucked away at the bottom of the backyard. It wasn't until many years later, when visiting Canada, America, England and European countries such as France, Switzerland and Austria that I found edible gardens where fragrant herbs and flowers were folded in with the fruit and vegetables — as in medieval gardens of long ago. These gardens are often referred to as 'potager' gardens; the word 'potager' is derived from the French word potage, which does not mean pots and pans, but a thick vegetable soup generously flavoured with herbs.

In recent years I have lived in Australia and New Zealand, where here, too, the concept of creating ornamental edible gardens — both productive and aesthetically pleasing — has been adopted wholeheartedly.

People the world over are now investing time and energy into lovingly tended vegetable gardens, sometimes even placing them at the front of the house. The pathway to the front door is a delicious assault on the senses — flanked by clumps of crops smothered in bees, made fragrant by the pungent sun-released oils of culinary herbs and colourful with flowers grown as companion plants, or simply for picking.

Gardens such as these, where aesthetics and practicality are combined to

Although this is an ornamental vegetable garden in the grand style, its basic design elements would adapt well to smaller scale home vegetable gardens.

Young apple trees espaliered over a four-sided ornamental archway will create a delicious edible arbour. The trees are underplanted with companion plantings of nasturtiums and chives.

Opposite page: Knot gardens incorporated hedging with different foliage types to produce interweaving colours. Green English box and silver-leafed cotton lavender are combined to create this stylish design which resembles a giant star.

create something which pleases both the gourmet gardener's palate and the creative gardener's palette, shaped the design of my subsequent edible gardens and led me to a study of the history of the ornamental vegetable garden and the writing of this book — a pleasure I wish to share with all gardeners.

This custom of growing vegetables, fruit, herbs and flowers in both an ornamental and utilitarian manner evolved in the monastery gardens and castle courtyards of medieval England and Europe. These modest plots were succeeded by the great gardens of wealthy landowners, and design for the foodstuff garden was eventually subject to the same degree of formality and aesthetics as the rest of the garden.

Travellers returning to Europe from the Americas in the sixteenth century brought with them exotic edible plants treasured for both their beauty and their culinary value. They brought back vegetables such as potatoes, tomatoes, aubergines/eggplants, French beans and pumpkins — arranging them in formal patterns in parterres, which was the prevailing style of gardening at this time. The beds themselves were strictly geometric in shape and often bordered by low hedges of clipped box (*Buxus sempervirens*), or by evergreen herbs such as lavender, rosemary or santolina (*S. chamaecyparissus*). Sometimes several different types of hedging were used to create the effect of interweaving colours and textures, and the fashion was for knot gardens or parterres of complicated design.

The plants and herbs were chosen not only for their food value but for their contrasting colours, size, leaf shape and texture, and carefully grouped accordingly to give maximum visual effect. The arrangement of the traditional edible garden was strictly symmetrical, and within the linear confines of its hedges and old brick walls, wicker support frames, twiggy tepees, trellises, fruit tunnels, topiary, espalier frames and arbours all combined to create an attractive setting for edible plants.

The most elaborate ornamental vegetable garden or potager in medieval times was the Potager du Roi at Versailles created for the 'Sun King', Louis XIV, by landscape gardener Jean-Baptiste de la Quintinie in 1683. The gardens have been maintained ever since as the world's most famous edible garden. La Quintinie developed the fruit-pruning systems that we still use today, and examples of many shapes and forms are still maintained at Versailles.

Internationally acclaimed potager gardens of more modern vintage are those of the Château de Villandry near Tours in France. Laid out around 1906 when the property was restored by Dr Joachim Carvallo, the kitchen garden covers 0.4 hectares (1 acre) divided into nine separate squares. These in turn are each divided into a highly individual pattern of edible and floral plantings.

In England, the grande dame of garden design, Rosemary Verey, created one of the first well-known potagers at her home in Barnsley House in

Gloucestershire. In addition to featuring rare edibles and innovative planting combinations, special features included an arbour covered with golden hops, and a tunnel that supported marrows flanked by giant sunflowers. Sweet peas and edible peas, some with two-tone lilac flowers, were trained up bamboo poles set diagonally across two small square beds in a cross pattern. Fruit trees were trained into espaliers and cordons of diverse forms.

When she died a decade ago at the age of 82, Rosemary Verey's designs for aesthetically pleasing and productive edible gardens had been replicated across Europe.

In other parts of the world, modern landscape artists continue to pioneer potager design: Canadian Patrick Lima's book *The Ornamental Edible Garden*, and in America, garden designer and landscaper Jennifer R Bartley's book *Designing the American Kitchen Garden — an American Potager Handbook* both feature a wealth of inspirational edible gardens.

In 2010, in Washington, DC, the United States Department of Agriculture established new ornamental edible gardens in the arboretum's National Herb Garden — with exhibits to tickle visitors' taste buds and to demonstrate ways in which gardeners can landscape with vegetable plants.

Grand edible gardens such as these are a living reminder that growing food need not always be a strictly utilitarian business. Although our present-day gardens are far removed from the grounds of French châteaux or

Knots &/or parterres

These two words are used interchangeably. Both types of garden were fashioned from three or more traditional plants, such as cotton lavender, silver germander and English box, chosen for the contrasting colours of their foliage. This combined with careful clipping created the illusion that the low-level hedges were 'knotted' or woven over or under each other rather than simply butting up against each other. The only difference between the terms 'knot garden' and 'parterre' is that although the same type of plants were used, the designs in the parterre were more complex and resembled a living embroidery — 'parterre de broderie'. The parterre garden was also generally larger than the simpler knot garden, and often contained elegant statuary and water features. It was designed to be seen from first floor rooms or terraces, whereas the knot garden was admired only at ground level. Many of these elaborate knot gardens and parterres still exist in France and other European countries today.

Filled with enriched soil and housing an attractive variety of herbs and vegetables with different foliage colour, form and textures, these stylish raised beds are perfect for small gardens. Their height makes for comfortable maintenance and harvesting of produce.

country estates, modern vegetable gardens show that the art of providing the household with an abundance of fruit, vegetables, herbs and flowers in a setting that is as attractive to the eye as the rest of the garden is enjoying an unprecedented revival.

Why plant an ornamental edible garden?

I hope this book will illustrate that the ornamental kitchen garden presents every creative gardener with an exciting challenge, that the end product — produce with pleasure — brings the bonus of home-grown, organically raised foodstuffs that have not been subjected to toxic sprays during growth.

The tired, cling-wrapped, asphyxiated salad stuffs and vegetables bought from the supermarket bear no resemblance to the fresh crunchy produce harvested from one's own garden.

Home-grown vegetables literally reacquaint one's taste buds with the true flavour of an edible plant, and in addition, the 'grow your own' philosophy brings with it the distinct advantage of economy on the home front.

Traditional old-fashioned stalwart vegetables are happily still with us, but seedsmen's catalogues worldwide also offer them in modern hybrid forms with fruit and foliage of exciting colours and textures. We have a wealth of produce of international origin — wonderful leafy vegetables from the orient for those who enjoy Asian cuisine, fabulous salad plants, baby gourmet vegetables as well as dwarf fruit trees, some of which bear not one but double or triple strains of fruit.

The form, colour and texture of vegetable foliage is extremely diverse and combined make for planting arrangements with striking visual appeal

— further enhanced by low borders of evergreen hedges or shrubby herbs. In addition, the more formal design of a classic ornamental edible garden is well suited to the smaller gardens of today, and plant breeders are continually hybridising mini edible vegetables for limited spaces and container cultivation.

The symmetrical confines of the modern potager are pleasing to the eye and maximise every bit of soil. Many vegetables such as beans and peas may be grown vertically on tepees, archways or frames, leaving valuable ground space free for crops of a more terrestrial growth habit. Even marrows, squash or courgettes/zucchini become focal points when suspended from an arch rather than hidden beneath foliage on the ground.

Soft fruit bushes may be trained as standards, and vines and fruit trees espaliered along walls or frames, fulfilling the dual role of pleasing design and providing maximum produce in minimum space. Conifers or box hedging plants clipped as topiary specimens, standardised lavender, rosemary or miniature roses look delightful combined with herbs and vegetables and enhance the pleasing symmetry of traditional edible garden design.

The vegetable garden of today is an exciting place where art and practicality have married: their offspring, a fabulous range of 'designer veg' that are easy to grow, visually pleasing, and exceptionally good to eat!

A colourful brick wall provides support for an espaliered apple. Walls such as this one encourage bumper crops by providing maximum warmth and shelter.

CHAPTER ONE

Planning & designing

The 'ground rules' advocated by Louis XIV's gardener, La Quintinie, as the basic practical requirements for a good potager are as relevant today as they were in medieval times.

> *'The ground chosen must be good whatever the Colour be and have a good convenience to water, the site should be set upon a small rising of which the weather situation must be favourable, design should be of an agreeable figure and all should be enclos'd with reasonably high walls, the access easy and convenient.'* Art of French Vegetable Gardening, *Louisa Jones (full details in bibliography).*

This famous gardener of long ago knew the value of providing a sheltered, sunny and free-draining site for the cultivation of edibles. Walls and hedges were designed to protect the garden from harsh winds, and to create a favoured micro-climate which would lead to extended growing periods.

Choosing the site

When choosing a site for an edible garden, it is important to keep in mind not only the vagaries of the weather but the geography and ambience of the garden as a whole. Will the potager be on show to visitors, and from what other vantage points in the garden will it be visible?

Will it be in clear view from the house windows or terrace — seen from above as a beautifully laid-out tapestry? Will it be presented as a main feature bordered only by dwarf hedges so that it will be open and dramatically displayed, or will it be concealed, walled and secret so that one comes upon it suddenly as a hidden treasure?

Above: This traditional potager of strong classical design features immaculately clipped dwarf hedges, enhancing the softer forms and colours of the vegetable foliage. A climbing bean in a terracotta pot makes a pleasing centrepiece and the fruit trees espaliered on Cotswold stone walls are underplanted with marrows and zucchinis.

Left: This newly developing edible garden features bold design concepts, interesting bed edgings and traditional fences and archways of woven willow prunings. The latter provide support for climbing beans later in the season. The handsome bay tree in the terracotta pot is underplanted with herbs and edged with santolina.

This ornamental edible garden is in the early stages of development and its basic design and layout can be clearly seen. Geometrically precise beds are neatly edged with timber and the L-shaped beds which mitre the corners are useful for plantings of soft fruit bushes, citrus or herbs. Although the basic ground plan is formal, the potager is enclosed with informal plantings of fruit trees, lavender and a curving box hedge. To the right, a stout trellis frame for the support of climbing crops or espaliered fruit creates a strong design feature.

Viewpoints & perspective

If your potager's design has a fairly simple geometric layout it will be easily seen from many viewpoints, so it should look pleasing from all angles. One ill-placed block of slow-growing broccoli, for example, will hide or detract from smaller, more colourful plants near or behind it for the whole season. If the potager is too large to be admired from one place, you'll need to plan for a series of viewing points.

This rule also applies if you want to grow a large variety of edible plants. Too many different varieties, even in one big picture, can create a messy overall view, so it's wiser to create a series of smaller pictures within the one large frame. With judicious planning you can place frames of espaliered fruit or vines, topiary specimens, hedges or screens to create a series of small garden rooms. This also adds a pleasant feeling of intimacy and surprise to the general ambience of the garden, making the observer wonder what is in the next area.

The natural places to pause in any garden are just inside the entrance, at the corners, the centre and at the junction of paths. People will also pause automatically at seats and even if they don't sit, they will stand here for a few moments to gaze at the garden as a whole. How well did you plan the planting of your garden? A good test is to walk immediately to all these places in your potager and see how pleasing they are to the eye.

If you've had to create your garden from an awkward shape and haven't been able to arrange the beds with the required symmetry, the answer (as with any less than desirable feature) is to make a focal point of any problem areas instead.

Plan for a really eye-catching crop to screen the difficult patch — a stand of tall sunflowers, a tepee of unusual runner beans, handsome clusters of fruit, beautiful or unusual vegetables, or crops imaginatively displayed — cucurbits suspended overhead, for example, instead of hidden on the ground beneath their leaves. Plantings such as these are visually pleasing and draw the attention away from unattractive areas and make ugly structures less obvious.

There are a number of other ways visitors might be encouraged to pause at favoured viewpoints or gaze in a particular direction. A central focal point such as a sundial, a circular bed, or a handsome topiary specimen in a container will cause feet to stray from a straight pathway. A short tunnel or archway framing an enticing glimpse of the garden invites immediate exploration. The same is true of any corner — the eyes and feet are drawn around the curve to discover what lies beyond.

In an area where there are mass plantings of low-growing crops, the contrast of vertical accents or a background framework may be provided with blocks of tall plants such as globe or Jerusalem artichokes, sweetcorn, burgundy-coloured amaranths, broad beans with scented black and white flowers, or sweet peas scrambling up a frame.

Although the design layout of this highly productive potager is basically formal, a sleepy scarecrow and luxuriant plantings of mixed flowers and vegetables impart a sense of fun. The apothecary's rose, *R. gallica officinalis*, underplanted with box makes an attractive focal point at centre.

Below: The design of this developing potager illustrates how dynamic the use of geometric shape can be in garden landscaping, and how a formal design may still be created in an awkward or irregular space.

The basic rule for creating focal points is that they should be in proportion to the scale of their surroundings. If the aim is to draw the eye to the end of a long axis, it will need to be large — a 2-m (7-ft) silvery cardoon in all its thistle-like glory, for example — or it will fade into the background. However, if you want to draw the eye to the central point of a small potager, the same cardoon, while still handsome, will now be threatening! A single standard lavender or rosemary bush would be a safer option in this case.

Suggestions for plantings with visual impact at lower levels might include a stand of red or gold rainbow chard, a block planting of golden courgettes/zucchini, or pumpkins of orange-red tangled through with dwarf nasturtiums of similar tonings.

As you can see, the permutations of planting for visual excitement are endless. Unlike 'hard' focal points such as statuary, plants change throughout their growth so that visual interest is constantly maintained. Take care, however, not to make too many dramatic statements; they'll either cancel each other out, or the overall effect will be overwhelming — the eye can be just as effectively drawn to a favoured area by a well-planned juxtaposition of bed shapes and the directions of rows within the beds.

This 'under construction' ornamental edible garden illustrates the challenging design principles required for establishing a garden on a steep site. The slope has been cut into terraces and raised beds shaped into the hillside have been formed from built-up layers of weathered railway sleepers.

Irregular or awkwardly shaped sites

If the only area you have available to create an edible garden is an awkward shape, it needn't necessarily prevent you from making a symmetrical pattern. You can achieve much by planning the plantings and the shape of your beds to balance the picture. With careful thought, especially for the edges of the plot, it will be possible to use all available cropping space without compromising the shape of your main pattern.

You can change squares and rectangles to rhomboids, adjust the length of L-shapes, or squash circles slightly on one side. This juggling will allow you to fit them into awkward spots but still align with your central axis. If possible, it's better to adjust the shape of the larger beds without it being obvious that you have done so. Employ a little native cunning by making the adjustment look like a deliberate manoeuvre rather than a mistake — for example, place vertical accent plants or structures strategically to distract the eye if you've had to bend a path that should be straight, or use planted containers to prevent someone from standing at a viewpoint from which uneven sides or angles are evident.

Steep sites

I am often asked if it is possible to create a potager on a steep, sloping site: in fact this is entirely possible since spatial definition and symmetry can be achieved just as well by a change of level as by a pattern of beds on a flat site.

The potager may be designed as a series of simple terraces, remembering the basic rule that the steeper the slope, the narrower the step. A drop of 45 cm (18 in) over 9 m (30 ft) can be converted to 3-m (10-ft) wide areas with three wooden barriers 15–20 cm (6–7 in) high, as long as these barriers are attached to stout stakes driven in at least 60 cm (2 ft) deep.

Provided there is a good depth of soil overall, there will be no restriction on what may be grown. It is not advisable to have a path at the top edge of each step, as walking too close to the edge may burst the barriers.

A terraced potager has several advantages: from above, the whole of the pattern makes an attractive tapestry; from ground level, you don't have to bend quite so far to pick plants on the edge of each step; and you can utilise the step edge to grow plants such as strawberries or dwarf beans which would otherwise need support to prevent their fruit trailing on the ground.

If you absolutely must have a perfect geometric shape to work with and feel there is one awkward area in the overall design that can't be disguised, the solution is a tall hedge or fence to screen it off. The space needn't be lost — it will still be useful for compost bins, stakes or toolshed and other less attractive gardening paraphernalia.

It is not always possible to choose the ideal site for one's garden, and overcoming the design challenges presented by a long narrow section is a common problem. The owner of this site has created the illusion of width by breaking it up into four individual beds and by not compromising on the generous six-brick span of the pathway, which gives an added feeling of breadth. The width of the beds is further maximised by plantings moving from low at the front to taller at the back.

Long, narrow sites

A common problem in the smaller rear garden of a modern home is that the site for a vegetable garden is usually long and narrow. Long beds aligned down a narrow garden make it look even narrower, so the perspective lines need to be adjusted to compensate for this. Here are a number of ways to create an illusion of width.

1. Plant rows of vegetables in solid blocks across the beds, rather than lengthways.

2. Create triangular beds with the apices pointing towards the entrance to the potager to provide a broadening effect.

3. Plant smaller plants at the front, progressing in size to larger ones at the back to reduce the impression of distance; the opposite progression will make a short garden appear longer.

4. Plan block plantings of taller plants with substantial body at the furthest point of the garden, or incorporate a strong focal point such as an archway, an espalier of fruit, a bold piece of statuary, clumps of soft-fruit bushes, tepees with climbing edibles, or any aspect offering a solid mass. The eye will traverse the length of the beds to the area of density, registering the illusion that the garden is broader than it really is.

Size

Having a small garden doesn't mean you can't have an attractive one; the tiniest of spaces, either rectangle or square, can be divided into four smaller beds (see Plan 6, page 20). An appealing arrangement of spring onions, dwarf beans, radishes, beetroot and lettuces planted in one of the plots can yield a surprisingly large harvest. With three other sections left to fill, there's still room for slow-to-mature larger plants such as main-crop potatoes, onions, parsnips, brassicas and leeks.

The ground plan of this edible garden illustrates that formal beds can be created from an irregular shape. Plantings in diagonal rows are bordered by dwarf hedges of box in a roughly triangular bed. A circular bed with white iris and a container planted with lavender forms a pleasing centrepiece.

Below: Clipped box hedges and sculptured topiary specimens create rectangular parterres of strong formal design. The garden beds contain a variety of fruit and vegetables, while the brick pathway draws the eye to the wooden archway at its end.

5. A row of standards, topiary specimens or other plants in containers, increasing in height as they get further away, will also have the effect of shortening the overall view.

6. If you choose to brick the pathways, lay the bricks sideways instead of longitudinally.

7. Create illusion with colour. To foreshorten a long, narrow garden, use plants with bright bold colours such as pot marigolds, nasturtiums, sunflowers or dahlias at the rear. The hot colours will 'come forward', giving the illusion that the garden is shorter in length than it really is. If you wish to make a short, narrow garden appear longer, plant the bright bold colours at the entrance and use blue-toned colours which have a receding effect at the rear. Vegetables with greyish green/blue foliage, such as cabbages, leeks, purple-leafed and podded dwarf beans, will create the illusion of distance.

Careful consideration of aspects such as these also emphasises the wisdom of putting pen to paper and planning before rushing out to create your potager. Remember, your aim is twofold — to create an edible garden that is not only productive, but also aesthetically pleasing.

Suitable shapes

La Quintinie's concern was as much for the pleasing proportions of the garden as for its productivity.

> 'The best figure for a Fruit or Kitchen garden and most convenient for Culture is a beautiful Square of straight angles, being once and a half if not twice as long as 'tis broad . . .' Art of French Vegetable Gardening, Qouise Jones (full details in bibliography)

What he advocates is, of course, a rectangle in modern gardeners' terminology. The entrance, he advises, should be placed in the short side of the design, facing a broad path extending the whole length of the potager.

Another favourite medieval ground plan, still used worldwide today, is to divide each square within the rectangle into two triangles, with the centre higher than the outside edges. Endless variations of plant texture, height and colour are possible within this basic design, and in the case of the more ornate layouts, you can use or adapt some of the suggested centrepiece ideas in the plans (see pages 18–21) to other, differently shaped, gardens.

For the beginner, the simplest design for a potager layout at ground level is a square or rectangle divided into four equal beds (see Plan 1, page 18) and edged with a low hedge of English box *Buxus sempervirens*, or with the shrub honeysuckle *Lonicera nitida* (mock box), which create neat, low hedges when clipped. A particularly attractive form of *Lonicera nitida* is the

golden-coloured cultivar 'Baggeson's Gold'. This cultivar is also effective used in combination with hedging plants of other foliage colours to create the illusion of woven or knotted hedges such as those created to enclose parterres and knot gardens. Evergreen herbs such as lavender, santolina or rosemary also make attractive hedging plants.

Within the beds, mangetout peas, French beans, salad greens and herbs may be mixed with new varieties of trusted old favourites — red Brussels sprouts, golden celery, purple-leafed leeks, red or gold-stemmed chards — all presenting a glorious variety of leaf shape, colour, size and texture.

A highly decorative potager in which repetitive concentric circles create an attractive circular ground plan. An urn containing a small figure is underplanted with herbs and white *Lychnis coronaria alba* to form an attractive centrepiece.

Plan 1: Diagonal row concept

This plan illustrates a simple but effective traditional potager design in which one large square is divided into four smaller squares. A further design option is to divide the latter into two triangular beds intersected with narrower pathways, which also avoids the necessity of walking on the soil, which can be a nuisance in wet weather.

The beds may be planted in diagonal rows with edibles of varying heights and colours which makes for interesting patterns and textures, or block-planted with cabbages, cauliflowers, broccoli, etc. The longest rows may be used for one's favourite vegetables and the shorter ones for others. The corners are ideal for single plants like courgettes, for clumps of herbs or vertically grown vegetables such as climbing beans. Main pathways should be a minimum of 1 m (3 ft) wide to allow barrow and easy working access.

The simple geometric layout of Plan 1 allows versatility and flexibility of design; a bowl effect may be achieved by planting the tallest vegetables and herbs on the outside and the lowest in the middle, or by putting them the other way round to create a pyramid effect. Similarly, even though the diagonal rows predominate, the inner corner of each of the four squares may be cut off to form a separate bed in the middle. Combined, these beds form a circle or diamond shape which will look attractive planted with different salad plants, a colourful patch of edible flowers, or if central height and vertical accent are required, with climbing vegetables on tepees.

Hedging plants — *Buxus sempervirens, Lonicera Nitida*

Pathways — brick, paving slabs, pebbles or shingle

Choosing & laying out the ground plan

The marking out of a knot or parterre garden isn't difficult but it is an exercise which requires care if the results are to look good in the years ahead. Choose one of the designs from the traditional ground plans on these pages and follow the instructions for marking it out on page 20. These plans are reasonably straightforward and can be set up without complicated geometric calculations. Basic tools required include wooden pegs and a ball of strong, non-stretching string. The design can be scratched into the ground, or marked with sand trickled out of a bottle.

The first set of lines to be marked out are for the outer frame. Next locate the centre point of the garden at the intersection of diagonal lines as they cross from opposite corners of the frame. Finally mark the lines that will make up the basic geometrical inner design.

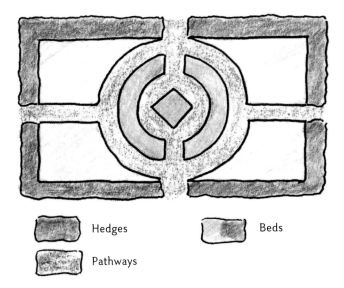

Hedges

Beds

Pathways

Plan 2: A circular design within a rectangle

Created from a rectangle, this plan offers an attractive circular design which becomes divided into a semicircle by the intersection of pathways for easy working and harvesting. The bed at the heart of the design can be another small circle to emphasise the concentric effect of the overall design, or diamond shaped to give an interesting geometric contrast.

Pathways

Beds

Plan 4: A 'three-in-one' layout

This elongated rectangle composed of three squares contains the basic ground-plan layout for one large and ornate potager, or for three separate designs. In each case, the basic geometry is of a square within a square intersected by a pattern of pathways for decorative and utilitarian effect.

Plan 3: Formed from a square or a rectangle

This is for a more ornate and larger potager and is formed equally well from either a square or a rectangle. The design allows for pathways for easy access to all beds. The central square offers an interesting combination of shapes and could be extracted from the larger design to create an attractive smaller potager.

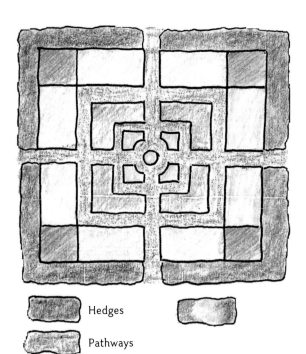

Hedges

Pathways

Plan 5: For a formal garden

Plan 6 features a ground plan with an interesting combination of geometric shapes within a large square. The four elongated rectangles at the outer edges of the potager offer scope for soft-fruit bushes or espaliered fruits and vines, or beds for herbs. Provision is made for space for a fruit tree at each of the four corners. As with Plan 3, the centre square extracted would make an attractive traditional potager design in its own right.

Plan 6: Traditional ground layouts for the potager

This illustrates a series of geometrical shapes such as squares, triangles and circles. By combining a series of these shapes, plots of any size can be given formality and structure. The centre of the ground plan, the circular design within the rectangle, could be extracted to form an interesting layout, or either of the two square plans standing alone would offer a parterre of traditional design.

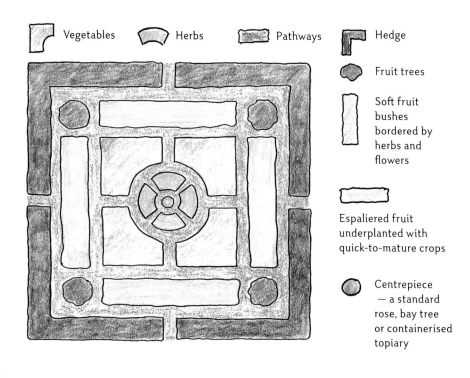

Vegetables   Herbs   Pathways   Hedge

Fruit trees

Soft fruit bushes bordered by herbs and flowers

Espaliered fruit underplanted with quick-to-mature crops

Centrepiece — a standard rose, bay tree or containerised topiary

Marking out the potager ground plan

Once you've chosen your basic design, draw the plan to scale on a sheet of graph paper. Prepare the area by digging it over, remove any perennial weeds and add manure or compost. Finally, rake the soil level. Transfer your design to the prepared area using a series of pegs and twine for the straight lines, and sand trickled from a bottle for the circles or curved lines. It's best to use sand because lines measured out and scratched into the earth can be washed away by a shower of rain.

With a square or rectangular shape, it's easy to check that the sides are exactly at right angles by measuring from corner to corner and adjusting if they are not equal in length. Find the centre point of the garden by running two lengths of twine from one corner across to the opposite corner so that they cross diagonally. Place a cane at the exact spot the lines meet in the middle. This cane should remain in position throughout, since it determines the position of all future measurements.

Tie another length of twine to this cane, to measure the exact circumference or dimensions for the centrepiece of the design. Extend the twine outwards around the cane and mark the outline of the desired shape for the centrepiece. If solid edgings are to be used along pathways, to prevent pebbles, gravel or softer pathway mediums from falling into the beds, make allowances for them at this stage (see Chapter 3, page 35).

Plan 7: A simple parterre

Medieval gardeners were always very formal in design, growing vegetables, herbs and flowers together in rectangular and circular beds. These designs adapt well to modern gardens where limited space makes informal design difficult. Knot gardens and parterres were popular in England and Europe as far back as the fifteenth century. Plan 7 is based on a medieval design for a simple parterre, and like all the basic ground-plan layouts in this section can be adapted in size to fit the largest or smallest of gardens.

An option for a more formal look would be to edge the beds to correspond with the outer hedge.

Knots & parterres

Knot gardens in ancient days resembled the designs on Persian and Indian carpets in their complexity, and incorporated different types of hedging to produce interweaving colours. The great potager gardens at Versailles and Villandry in France have many such parterres, but this sort of thing may be a bit over the top for the modern home edible garden! It's wiser to settle for a simple design, especially if you're planning to grow herbs, flowers and vegetables together within one parterre.

Traditional hedging plants for this type of knot garden include grey-foliaged *Santolina chamaecyparissus*, silver germander (*Teucrium fruticans*), dark green box (*Buxus sempervirens*) and gold *Lonicera nitida* 'Baggeson's Gold'.

Young hedging plants should be grown about 15 cm (6 in) apart. Pinch out developing shoots to encourage the bushy growth required to form a dwarf hedge.

When the pathways have been constructed, the hedging plants should be set 15–25 cm (6–10 in) apart along the outlines of the design marked by sand and strings. Once the linear confines have been completed, you are ready to plan what shapes you want the beds to be before starting to dig them over.

Choosing the right shape for your beds

Making a template for repeated bed shapes

If you wish to build up a design with a repeated pattern of small beds of the same shape and size, such as a series of diamond shapes within a large circle, or a number of squares within a rectangle, it's worth taking the time to make a template. Draw the shape to actual size onto a large piece of cardboard, wood or plastic, with the digging area outlined in the middle. Obviously it would not be practical to try to make templates for large beds.

The template will be particularly useful if the beds are to be cut out of a grassed area. Peg the template in position on the ground and cut round the inside edges with a spade before removing the turf.

Brick pathways outline a
ground-plan design composed
of two square beds enclosed
by two L-shaped beds. The
inner beds are intersected with
narrower brick pathways for
ease of access and harvesting.
An ornamental archway planted
with the climbing rose 'Phyllis
Bide' spans the main pathway
through the edible garden, and
espalier fences divide the front
garden from the rear.

Tricky triangles & diamonds

A small triangle-shaped bed
serves the purpose of housing
three tepee poles for climbing
edibles. In general, small
triangles are best used for block
plantings. The more acute the
angles, the more difficult it is
to plant them so they maintain
their shape. The acute angle
needs to be filled with plants
that don't flop about, so you
must either provide support, or
use small plants such as salad
stuffs. The same problems
apply to elongated diamonds
or lozenge shapes; they have
acutely awkward angles to fill
unless the aim is for a tapestry
effect of plants in solid blocks.

Squares are easy

When it comes to the actual shape of beds, as the plans 1, 3 and 5 on pages
18, 19 and 20 show, squares are the easiest to work with. If the garden itself is
square, it can be divided into smaller squares, but also triangles, rectangles,
L-shapes or any combination of these shapes. Each of the four squares within
the main square allows plenty of planting scope.

Even a square with 1-m (3-ft) sides could be a mini-potager of its own,
with a 30-cm (1-ft) square of medium-tall plants such as broad beans,
Florence fennel or a single tomato in the middle, and two 15-cm (6-in)
wide rows of lower plants such as lettuces, carrots or beetroot. Or it could
have climbing edibles on tepees in each corner. A bed this size will provide
enough nutrients for six runner beans, four tomatoes or cucumbers, with a
quick crop of radishes or lettuces picked before they're overshadowed by
the beans.

L-shapes

L-shapes are much more useful and easy to handle. They can be thick or thin,
equal or unequally sided, and they fit neatly round a square or a rectangle as
shown in ground plans 3 and 4, page 19. Two of them will interlock with each
other to make a T-shape, or four back to back will make a cross. In essence,

This ornamental edible garden, established within an open lawn, has to look good from all angles. The garden is also viewed from the terrace and house above, so taking time in the initial stages to plan for block plantings and foliage combinations which will present a pleasing tapestry effect is well worth the effort.

they're really two rectangles joined together and so can be planted with interesting variations on any of the rectangular themes.

The only difficulty with L-shapes is how to get long rows around corners if you don't wish to mitre the corner. The best alternative is to make the corner into a separate square as in plans 3 and 4. The planting of a taller plant such as a tomato, or a tepee of climbing beans, will give vertical accent and create a focal point, and the original row of vegetables can be continued on the other side.

Rectangles

Rectangles, like squares, are easy shapes to deal with, from both the pattern planning and planting aspects. Two rectangles of identical size could be used without any other shapes to make a complete edible garden. This idea has merit because one is dealing with a known quantity all the time when digging, manuring or planting. The rectangles can be planted with masses, blocks or rows, and the rows can be long, short or diagonal. Two rectangles alongside each other with opposite diagonal rows would make a herringbone pattern, or a series of rectangles could be used to make other herringbone patterns. Intersected with paths of bricks laid in a pleasing pattern, this simple design is one that has maintained its popularity from medieval times.

Curved beds

All the beds discussed so far have straight sides. There's no reason why beds with curved sides shouldn't be employed but they're best filled with block plantings because it can be difficult to deal with curved rows in any other way. Curved patterns may be created, and if edibles are planted to touch but not overwhelm each other, the outer leaves will form a moisture-saving and weed-suppressing ground cover. Block planting also offers the option of creating a chequerboard effect by using alternate plants of different colours, perhaps red and gold beetroot, or green and purple dwarf beans, or mixed lettuces in shades of red and green.

CHAPTER TWO

Constructing the framework

Now for the hard stuff — the 'hardscaping' of the solid and permanent areas of your edible garden. This includes planning and constructing pathways and edgings, paved walking and working areas, and the erection of permanent support structures and frames for climbing vegetables, vines and fruit as well as the laying of foundations for ornamental structures and statuary.

Pathways & edgings

Suitable mediums for pathways include bricks, pavers, concrete slabs, gravel, pea shingle, pebbles, bark and grass to provide a firm base for easy access to the beds for maintenance and harvesting. Gravel, scoria, bark or crushed oyster shell are less expensive than bricks or custom-made pavers, but allow weed growth and will eventually break down and need replacing. Grass pathways require regular mowing so make sure they are wide enough for the width of the mower you will be using. They are, however, labour intensive and become worn and muddy in wet weather. In general, all paths should be a minimum of 1 m (3 ft) for wheelbarrow access and comfortable walking.

Bricks are the traditional paving medium for potager pathways and walls — they're also long lasting and attractive — but can be costly. Second-hand, uncleaned bricks with mortar and cement still attached are inexpensive but entail long hours with chisel, hammer and scrapers to remove the old mortar, but the aged, mellow ambience they give when laid is (probably) worth it.

If you're content to use modern custom-made bricks, the price (ironically) is a little less than for demolition bricks, and they soon mellow to the softer tones of the latter. If a less than flourishing bank account prohibits the use of bricks, and less noble materials, like concrete blocks or paving, must be used, their harsher facades can be softened with creeping thymes and sedums.

Pathways made with softer mediums must have a solid edging, or the bark, pebbles, shingle or oyster shell will fall into the beds. Railway sleepers are strong, long-lasting and aesthetically pleasing. Demolition yards offer timbers such as floor or skirting boards which make sturdy edgings of good height, but ensure they're in good condition and pleasing to look at. Custom-made lengths of jointed and ribbed wooden gardening edging also make effective dividers for pathways and beds, and will weather to an attractive patina. Brick, stone or slab pathways look best edged with bricks or tiles in a slanted vertical position, but rows of upright bricks laid side by side also look attractive.

Old bricks of irregular shapes create the pathway in this appealing ornamental edible garden. In order to maintain the path at consistent width, the bricks have been spaced with mortar and bordered on the outer edge with others of regular size laid end to end.

Dimensions

When you're planning the dimensions of your paths, remember that bricks and most paving slabs come in standard sizes. Decide which medium you prefer, and in what pattern, then check sizes and required spacing to arrive at the final width. If you are going to be laying bricks or pavers yourself, invest in a pair of padded strap-on knee pads. I laid pathways in my edible garden involving some 2000 bricks and even with deluxe pads had, in the end, to restrict myself to laying 50–60 bricks (about 1 m, 3 ft) per day!

Flanked by borders of fruit and vegetables, black and white pebbles laid in swirling designs and set into a solid base create an intriguing and inviting pathway.

Preparation — framing up the pathway

Whether your finished design has solid edgings or not, all pathways need constructing within an initial framework first. Using wooden pegs and twine, measure out the dimensions of the paths and dig them out, then level and flatten. Hammer in the wooden pegs at regular intervals along the pathway and lay durable strips of timber inside them and nail together. Set the desired pathway within this frame.

Laying paving slabs

Paving slabs need to be embedded in mortar, a mixture of cement and lime or both, with sand and water used to hold the bricks or stones together.

Having excavated and levelled the area to be paved, put down a layer of hardcore (brick rubble or broken concrete). Use a tamper or roller to crush it flat. Then use a section of plank to spread a layer of ash, lean mix concrete (one part cement to three to four parts sand) or similar fine material over the hardcore to bind it together. Trowel the mortar over the area for the first

Laying a brick pathway

Once the outer framework of your brick path is firmly in place, put down approximately 7 cm (2¼ in) of 'hardcore' (brick rubble or broken concrete), which must be compacted by rolling and stamping, then a layer of sand or 'lean mix' – about three to four parts of sand to one of cement. Lay the bricks or slabs on top in the desired pattern, using a spirit level to check that they are level, then fill the gaps with dry lean mix, brushing it firmly into all the cracks.

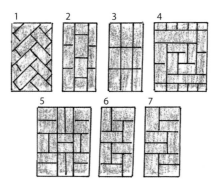

Brick patterns

Bricks can be laid flat or on edge, in straight rows or various patterns. Since a standard brick is half as wide as it is long, there are a number of easy patterns involving blocks of two or three bricks. These are known as basketweave, and allow an easy calculation of widths. One of the most elegant patterns is herringbone (1), but it is more difficult to lay since it involves skilful cutting to fill in the small triangles at the edges.

Aromatic pathways

Herbs such as creeping thymes or chamomiles, which release their pungent perfumes when trodden on, are so delightful it's worth having them, even if you have to hand-weed them occasionally. Unlike grass pathways, they don't require mowing, but need solid edgings to prevent them 'creeping' into beds.

slab. Ensure that it is spread to the correct height. To ensure even spacing between slabs temporarily insert pieces of wood of uniform size and width. Tap the slabs into the desired position, using a spirit level to check that each one is level.

Laying pathways of shingle, bark, scoria, pebbles, gravel

If you choose one of these softer walking mediums, follow the construction processes for solid edgings, and when the pathway is dug out and levelled, remove all perennial weeds. Lay sheets of heavy-duty polythene to prevent regrowth and fill with the desired medium.

Raised beds

Problems common to many vegetable gardens include impoverished soil and poor drainage, but these can be easily overcome by creating raised beds — a design made popular by Austrian horticulturist Rudolph Steiner, who instituted them in Switzerland around 1900. The beds are filled with compost and manure-enriched soil. The height of the beds and the loose structure of the conditioned soil promote free drainage and healthy plant growth. Edging mediums for raised beds can include old railway sleepers, round poles, breeze blocks, or lengths of durable timber. The size, height and shape of the beds depends upon individual requirements.

Above: Cleverly designed on a sloping site, this developing edible garden features an inviting pergola and terraced levels with tiers of raised beds formed from railway sleepers.

Above, right: Raised beds formed from two levels of round poles hold a wide variety of herbs and vegetables. Wide pathways of grey gravel allow easy access for maintenance and harvesting of produce.

Opposite page, left: An archway of lashed bamboo canes and a frame to the rear left fulfil the dual roles of providing vertical accents and attractive support structures for sweet peas, nasturtiums and other climbing crops.

Building raised beds

Construction of raised beds isn't difficult, but requires accurate measurement and cutting of corresponding lengths of wood, some long strong nails for corner joints and a few wooden reinforcing pegs if long planks are being used. If round poles are going to be stacked vertically as an edging, nailing may be difficult; it's usually easier to wire them together.

Vertical accents & ornamental structures

In times past, the utilitarian vegetable plot tended to be basic, monotonous and horizontal, with all plantings laid out in rigid rows. Modern vegetable gardeners, however, have a delightful choice of ornamental structures and plant material at their disposal so that a happy balance between simplicity and variety is easily achieved.

While you might think of a vegetable garden as just a broad, flat bed with a mosaic of plants growing in it, gardens, in fact, are three dimensional. Plants growing at contrasting heights to show above and set off the ground level mosaic patterning will help achieve maximum ornamental effect. The garden's walls and hedges already provide vertical presence, but this needs to be emphasised by other upright structures, including temporary plants (tall edibles, such as globe artichokes, sweetcorn, climbing beans, tall growing herbs, etc.) or semi-permanent

constructions, such as plant supports or espalier frames.

These features are both ornamental and provide vertical accent, as do statues, sundials, fountains, bird baths and topiary in containers. Placed at the centre, beginning or end of converging pathways, or at entrances or exits, these structures are excellent for marking an axis or vista.

In countries where winters are severe, vertical accents might include citrus or dwarf fruit trees in large containers that can be moved into sheltered positions or covered with frost protection cloth when necessary. (See Chapter 5, Fruit in the edible garden, pages 83–93.)

Vines bearing edible fruit, or climbing roses on archways or pergolas, also make delightful vertical structures which enhance and improve the aesthetics of the garden.

Top: Dwarf lemon trees make attractive and productive container specimens and provide pleasing accent points along the pathway.

Above: Stone pavers set in gravel and edged with weathered sleepers create both bold design features and a strong framework in the centre of this small ornamental edible garden.

Vertical bamboo canes lashed together across a horizontal central runner create a support frame for climbing beans. To the right old-fashioned purple sweet peas grow over a series of ornamental metal hoops.

Below: Climbing beans scramble over a metal archway to create an attractive focal point. Sturdy archways such as this provide support for a wide variety of climbing fruit, vegetables and vines.

Structural supports for veggies

Medium-height plants, such as tomatoes, can be tied to wires, netting or mesh stretched between two posts — and larger varieties grown inside a cylinder of wire or plastic mesh attached to a single post.

The delicate tendrils of taller varieties of peas will cling to plastic or wire mesh but traditional pea and bean-sticks comprised of vertical rows of twiggy branches are both decorative and efficient.

Other useful plant supports include free-standing frames (of varying sizes) of wire netting stretched between battens, each with a leg at the back to support the frame at an angle. These are particularly useful for cucumbers or zucchinis which otherwise ramble over wide areas. Lower growing plants which dangle their fruits on the ground are best supported by a bamboo pole running horizontally each side of the row, raised to the appropriate height with bricks or blocks of wood. Although tunnels of wire netting are often suggested as good supports for low plants, it can be difficult to weed and pick fruit growing inside the netting.

Wherever poles or stakes are used, avoid them looking unsightly by 'blunting' the top with coloured tennis balls or small flowerpots or, with aesthetics in mind, splash out on ceramic figures designed specifically for this purpose.

Constructing frames
Basic support frames

To construct a basic support frame for climbing vegetables, or a frame on which to train espaliered fruit trees or vines, you'll need the following materials and tools.

- 4 or more (depending on length of frame required) stout 60 x 80 mm (2 in x 3 in) posts
- Strong wire
- Strong hooks with enclosed eyes
- Bamboo canes or lightweight twiggy tree branches
- Drill with a fine bit
- Pliers
- Post-hole borer or spade
- Mallet

Drill evenly spaced holes in the end posts and screw an eye hook into each. Drill holes at levels corresponding to those made in the edge posts for the eye hooks in the centre posts through which to thread the wire. You will need between 6–8 vertical rows placed approximately 18 cm (7 in) apart to make a waist-high frame. If the frame is to espalier fruit, support a vine

or form a concealing vegetative boundary, the hooks can be placed much further apart, but the supporting wooden posts will need to be taller.

Sink the posts firmly into the ground at regularly spaced intervals. Thread the wire through the hooks, then through holes in centre posts and strain it to get a firm tension. Sink bamboo canes or twiggy branches either side of the wires to give the climbing vegetables added support, and to help train the shape of young fruit trees. Frames can be removed as the branches of the young trees mature enough to fan out along the wires.

If a really tall strong frame is required, it's best to use custom-made steel posts that have holes already drilled in them for the insertion of wire. They're not so aesthetically pleasing in an ornamental vegetable garden but, unlike wooden posts, will last much longer as they don't rot.

(See Chapter 3 pages 40–41 for methods of training fruit trees as cordons or espaliers).

A number of ornamental structural supports are featured in this large formal garden, including twin tepees of stout wooden sticks to maximise planting space in the front bed.

The prolific small rose 'Phyllis Bide' scrambles up the metal archways marking the entrance and exit of this edible garden. Vegetable beds on the right are bordered by espaliered fruit trees on a post-and-wire frame such as that described on pages 40–41. Espalier frames not only maximise cropping in minimum space but create useful dividing elements between different garden areas.

Opposite page: Standing guard over fruit, flowers and vegetables, a couple of pot-person scarecrows bring a sense of fun to this highly productive edible garden.

Tepees, towers & archways

Twiggy branches stuck firmly into the ground with their tops arched inwards to form a vault, also make inexpensive, efficient and attractive supports for peas and beans. A similar classic support is a tepee of tall bamboo stakes tied together at the top, or you can build a tepee tower using four wooden stakes screwed together at the top and reinforced by wooden cross pieces at the base. This makes a permanent or long-lasting structure that can be moved wherever and whenever seasonal or planting plans dictate. It can also be used to support permanent plantings such as climbers, vines or roses. To ensure the wooden tepee doesn't topple under the weight of the crop or in high wind, peg the base down with heavy-duty, long-length tent pegs, crossing two at each corner.

The basic four-wooden-stake design, which is adequate for crops such as climbing beans, can be enhanced with trellis panels to give added support to cucurbits or other more ornamental climbers. The tepee may also be placed in a

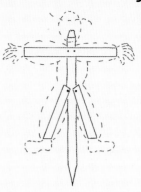

Scarecrows

Another way to provide decorative vertical interest in the edible garden, which is fun, is with scarecrows — mock human figures employed since medieval times to scare birds away from crops. Build the simple wooden 'body' frames below and let the family use their imagination in dressing them. Recently, my grandchildren created a 'Phantom of the Opera' figure with dashing red cloak (old bedspread), but the scarecrow which amused visitors most was a punk figure with spiked and aerosol-sprayed multicoloured straw hair, sunglasses and a pig ring through its nose! Make the framework for the scarecrow from pieces of old timber, but the centre stake must be sturdy enough to be hammered into the ground and tanalised for durability. The head can be made from flesh-coloured fabric or the waist section of old panty hose and stuffed with hay or straw. Hammer the skeleton (see diagram) firmly into the ground, place the head on top of the stake, dress the scarecrow and stuff garments with hay or straw. Tie ends of the sleeves and pants to stop the stuffing falling out.

wooden planter box or half barrel for container plantings where space is limited.

If there is a handyperson in the family, bribe him or her to put together a series of these tripods in varying heights and widths. If there is no handyperson available, give it a try yourself — I've managed to build several of varying sizes and the basic design can be scaled down to accommodate perennials. If painted in colours to match specific plants or areas of the garden, the tripods look upmarket and expensive though they cost little to produce. Screw a wooden ball or finial on top for the ultimate in elegance!

The beauty of growing 'vertical veg' is that the ground beneath the tripods can be planted with lower-growing edibles which won't interfere with the pea or bean crop above.

A pleasing natural-looking archway can be constructed by positioning two stands of slender pliable branches (willow is a traditional favourite) opposite each other and then bending and tying their tops together overhead.

CHAPTER THREE

Enclosing the edible garden

Successful vegetable gardening requires a site which offers maximum sunshine but also protection from prevailing winds; in essence, a clever combination of exposure and enclosure — so a wall, fence or hedging along at least one or all four sides of the garden will be needed. Many gardeners would love a vegetable garden enclosed by mellow brick walls like those of ancient potagers, but be aware that a wall of even modest proportions takes an astonishing amount of costly bricks, and while laying a brick pathway is well within the capabilities of the home gardener, laying a wall takes professional skill and expertise.

Walls & other enclosures

Traditional enclosures include brick walls, hedges, picket or wooden fences, cordons of fruit or vines trained on wires or frames, and stands of soft-fruit bushes. In addition to providing shelter, solid enclosures offer the bonus of providing support for climbing edibles and also increase the productive surface of the garden since vertical planting can be practised. Less permanent plantings, like melons, squashes and cucumbers, are easily trained on netting, frames and trellises or against a solid vertical support.

Gates

Walled and ornamental vegetable gardens are further enhanced by entrances featuring ornamental gateways. Wrought-iron and aluminium lacework gates are attractive, if costly, but once purchased last indefinitely. However, a little imagination, a visit to an auction, or a foray through demolition yards

Above: Closely woven twiggy prunings lashed to an outer framework of stout branches create an archway for this edible garden. Tall bottlebrush trees (*Callistemon* spp.) provide a colourful and unusual hedge and smaller plants in the garden are sheltered by beds of luxuriant-looking broad beans.

Above, right: Fashioned from lengths of wood, rustic wooden gates provide a strong design feature, in juxtaposition to the discreet wire fences enclosing the garden.

Left: The mellow Cotswold stone walls enclosing this grand formal potager also provide support for espaliered fruit.

Frames of willow prunings woven in a traditional manner enclose this edible garden. An archway of lashed wood will support climbing crops later in the season.

Below: In this informal edible garden vegetable beds are enclosed with a strong outer edging of scoured stones and a softer plant edging of forget-me-nots within. The potager is well protected by hedges of mature shrubs and trees.

can yield inexpensive gates of both wood and metal that make innovative additions to the potager. The head and foot of an old iron bedstead placed at the entrance and exit of an elongated brick pathway can draw the eye along a pleasing and dramatic vista. During a recent holiday in France I visited a potager approached through a wooden gate with palings arranged in graduating height to create a semi-circle at the top. The circle was completed by the addition of a semicircular arch of wood joined to the gate posts, thus framing the garden and drawing the eye through the circle to a sweeping view of the garden beyond. The basic design, simple enough for any (fairly!) handy gardener to construct, painted a subtle grey-green, made an elegant and unusual entrance to this garden.

Archways

Well-established potagers often have archways cut through mature hedges of yew, macrocarpa, hornbeam or beech. But if you're creating a new ornamental vegetable garden (and don't have half a century or so to spare), you'll have to settle for an archway of decorative trellis of metal or timber, or a hedge created from a quick-growing species through which you cut an archway. Trellis frames come in standard sizes with patterning of squares, diamonds and diagonals. If you prefer a more natural look, the garden may also be enclosed with archways of bent willow branches or tall twiggy prunings woven into a vaulted arch, as detailed in Chapter 2, pages 32–33.

Temporary enclosures or dividers

Taller vegetables, such as sweetcorn, cardoons, globe and Jerusalem artichokes, amaranths, broad beans and sunflowers, and taller herbs such as angelica, bronze fennel and borage, make attractive temporary screens or enclosures. Stands of climbing beans and peas can easily form a curtain between areas of the edible garden. Grown on twiggy branches or tripods they also form an attractive centrepiece. Topiary specimens or standardised lavender, rosemary, bay trees, dwarf fruit trees, citrus, etc., in containers, may also be used as instant screens or dividers. Chapter 7, pages 115–117 has information on pruning and shaping topiary forms and standards.

Aromatic & flowering edgings for beds & paths

The use of plants as low hedges along paths or around beds is traditional in potager design. These can be temporary and seasonal, e.g., parsley, beetroot, red and green basil, red-leafed lettuces or marigolds, etc., or more permanent with evergreen herbs such as lavender, blue-flowered rosemary, hyssop, or of silvery cotton lavender or helichrysums. These hardy shrubby herbs give sterling service, but can be short-lived, become woody and sparse or suffer die back. It's

Enclosed to the left by a tall hedge of dark green privet, the pathway of this formal edible garden is spanned by a hooped ornamental metal archway draped with sweet peas. Lower hedges of box-enclosed beds to the right and pathways of cream shingle complement the darker foliage of the privet and box.

Below: Vegetable beds are edged with luxuriant borders of lavender on their inner edges and with neat balls of box on the outer. In addition to providing symmetry, standard gooseberry bushes either side of the path create an attractive and unusual design feature.

irritating when one plant dies out, giving the hedge a gap-toothed appearance, but all grow easily from cuttings. Planted in the gap, they soon root to produce a new plant. An even quicker solution is to keep a supply of potted-up, rooted cuttings as a standby to use as instant replacement plants.

Colourful edging combos

- For a pleasing colour scheme of plum-purple, pewter and silver, combine a foliage edging of purple-leafed sage, *Salvia officinalis*, with a lilac-flowered lavender interspersed with clumps of chives with rosy-mauve ball heads.
- Rosemary (*Rosmarinus officinalis*) makes a hardy evergreen edging and clips into a neat, compact hedge. It also produces delightful silvery-blue flowers in winter when little else is in bloom.
- Silver germander (*Teucrium fruticans*) also clips into an attractive blue-flowered hedge. Grows quickly and needs fairly regular clipping. Requires good drainage.
- Lavender (*Lavandula angustifolia*) is a traditional favourite among the huge range available. It also comes as *L. a.* 'Alba' and *L. a.* 'Rosea', but they're less hardy than their robust blue-flowered relatives. *L. stoechas pedunculata*, with fat purple-blue spikes, adapts to most soils and even copes with poorly drained clay. For low edges or hedges, *L. angustifolia* comes in dwarf cultivars such as *L. a.* 'Hidcote', *L. a.* 'Loddon Pink', *L. a.* 'Nana Alba' and *L. a.* 'Munstead'.
- French lavender (*L. dentata*) is an excellent edger when a taller hedge

This large formal potager is enclosed by a beautifully sculpted hedge of pittosporum, *Pittosporum* 'Karo', trained at the centre into an attractive archway. Bold topiary forms of clipped box combine with the clean lines of the beds to create a potager of strong design and restful simplicity.

Opposite page: Common box, *Buxus sempervirens*, forms the framework for this edible garden and constitutes a strong design feature. The smaller variety, *B.* 'Suffruticosa', has been used for dwarf hedgings and edgings.

Temporary edgers

Certain vegetables and fruits can be used as interesting temporary edgings and outliners: over small areas, my favourites include dwarf varieties of vibrant red, gold and green capsicum and chilli peppers; and a border of strawberries delights as an easily harvested edging alongside a pathway. Herbs, and medicinal and aromatic companion plants also make exciting edgers. Chives, for example, with their lavender pom-pom flower heads, feverfew with daisy-like flowers, or massed herbs provide both attractive and insect-repelling edgings.

is required. Attractive and robust in growth, it is a hardy plant with grey-green foliage and soft lavender-blue flower spikes borne over long periods. In temperate zones, if kept lightly trimmed, it will flower almost year-round. Modern hybridists have also bred many other lavender cultivars designed to withstand climatic extremes.

- Santolina (*Santolina chamaecyparissus*) is also called cotton lavender but it isn't a true lavender. This dainty shrub has finely dissected silver foliage and clusters of golden ball-like flowers. It grows to a height of 70 cm (2 ft 3 in) and is cold hardy.

All four of these hardy herbs are daughters of sun-baked Mediterranean slopes and abhor wet feet. They'll tolerate poor soils but require full sun and good drainage, so it's wise to plant thirsty edibles such as tomatoes and leafy salad stuffs in inner beds rather than immediately beneath herb hedges.

Plant-edgers can be complemented by the types of plants chosen to grow behind them. Feathery, clear-green carrot foliage, for example, mixed with red oak-leaf lettuce or variegated thyme creates a pleasing tiered effect with its mix of varying leaf textures and colour tones.

Hedges

If a new edible garden is planned on an exposed site the best way to provide permanent protection is to plant a taller hedge. You can create an innovative living wall by planting a shelter belt of mixed evergreen and deciduous shrubs and trees, which will provide not only a wind screen but flowers and fruit as well. Vegetative windbreaks filter, absorb and deflect wind energy; the most effective plantings are those that modify the wind's force, rather than those forming an impenetrable barrier. When the wind is totally deflected by a solid fence or wall, it can cause severe erosion and turbulence in adjacent areas. There is also the danger that as plants top the fence they'll receive the full force of the wind, suffer root rock or have their heads torn off.

In all but coldest climates, a mix of hardy plants such as abelia, colutea, buddleia (will bring the butterflies), coprosmas, conifers, pittosporums, photinia, dogwoods (coloured stems in winter), cotoneasters (polished red or yellow berries), corokias, akeake (*Dodonaea viscosa*), hebes, elaeagnus, mahonia, pyracantha, phormiums and many others will provide effective outer shelter for the vegetable garden.

In Europe and North America, where harsh winters prevail, hardy and cold-tolerant evergreen hedging plants are required. These might include the yew (*Taxus baccata*), *Ligustrum japonicum*, *Viburnum tinus*, bay (*Laurus nobilis*), holly (*Ilex* spp.), pines (*pinus* spp.), conifers (*conifer* spp.) and the *Thuja* spp., which are also members of the conifer family. The latter have attractive aromatic foliage of yellow, bronze or green borne on spreading branches. Nurseries in both northern and southern hemispheres and in North America offer a wide variety of hardy conifer cultivars specifically bred for creating hedges and shelter belt protection.

Deciduous hedging plants include slow-growing hornbeam (*Carpinus* spp.) and beech (*Fagus* spp.).

This list is not exhaustive, but remember to include a good mix of evergreen varieties amongst the deciduous to ensure year-round shelter. Once an outer framework of shelter is established, the dwarf hedging to enclose vegetable beds can be planted.

Traditional dwarf hedges

If you have your heart set on dwarf hedges and despair because you need 400 plants, the shrub honeysuckle 'mock' box (*Lonicera nitida*) makes an attractive and quick-growing substitute for traditional box hedging (*Buxus sempervirens*). A pleasing golden variety, 'Baggeson's Gold' is available. *Lonicera* bears very dense small leaves, is hardy and grows easily from cuttings. English box (*Buxus sempervirens*) is the traditional dwarf hedging for the ornamental edible garden. Box is a small shrub with glossy dark green foliage, height 50 cm (20 in). The variety 'Suffruticosa' (edging box) grows to 25 cm (10 in). Recommended spacing distance for most shrubby hedging plants is 15–20 cm (6–8 in).

Taking box or *lonicera* cuttings for dwarf hedging

Take softwood cuttings from box or *lonicera* in late summer. Choose strong young shoots from the current year's growth. Take a length of about 7.5–10 cm (3–4 in) and cut just above a leaf joint, which is the best rooting area.

Both box and *lonicera* cuttings root readily, but a dip in hormone-rooting powder will speed up the process. Place cuttings into a mix of 50:50 peat and vermiculite, or three parts sand to one of potting mix. Water well, cover with polythene and place in a shady position. They should root in around eight weeks.

In small space or no-soil edible gardens, such as on verandahs, containers of dwarf citrus, olives and fruit trees make productive and attractive temporary or semi-permanent hedges and dividers.

Fruit trees trained to cordon or espalier forms on wire frames facilitate easy pruning, spraying and harvesting and allow maximum cropping in a minimal area.

Cordons

The term cordon refers to the main trunk of a tree from which the head has been removed and either one or two lateral branches allowed to grow horizontally beneath. A single cordon allows one branch to grow sideways and a double cordon allows two lateral branches to grow horizontally off the main trunk. Because the head is cut out of the tree when it is around 40 cm (15½ in) tall, the cordon specimen remains low in height. Although the cordon, like the espalier, is trained to grow flat against a wall or frame, because of its modest height it can remain free-standing.

Almost all varieties of apples, pears, plums, peaches and nectarines, and many other fruiting trees, can be trained as cordons, and also soft fruits such as gooseberry and red and white currants. There is a certain apprehension about training fruit trees as cordons and espaliers, but it is not difficult. All that is required is structural support and a well-fed, well-drained piece of soil in a sunny, sheltered position. For the tiny-space potager the single and double cordons are most suitable and simple for the beginner to manage.

Fruit trees as espaliers & cordons

Fruit trees are traditionally grown on frames, fences or walls in the potager as espaliers or cordons. They create garden 'rooms', dividers or green 'walls' and provide maximum crops in minimum space. The cordon, or espalier, is a tree which is trained to grow flat against a fence or wall from a single stem.

How to espalier, or cordon, fruit trees

Drive metal posts of about 3 m (10 ft) long, 65 cm (2 ft 2 in) into the ground at regular intervals to fill the space you want to use, but no closer that 45 cm (18 in) apart. This means that you can grow an interesting variety of fruit along a wall only 6 m (20 ft) long (see Chapter 5, pages 83–93, for suitable fruiting vines, trees and bushes). Stretch a wire from one post to the other at a level 45 cm (18 in) above the ground. Stretch two more pieces of wire above the first wire at a distance of approximately 65 cm (2 ft 2 in) from each other.

In selecting a young fruit tree to create a cordon, choose a self-fertilising

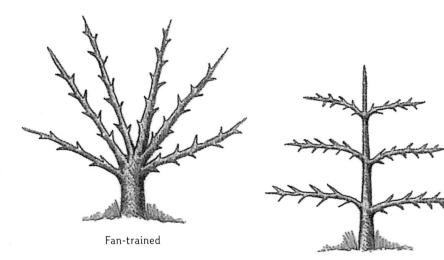

Fan-trained

Espalier, or horizontally trained

variety. Cut back to about 25 cm (10 in) from the ground after planting. Several shoots will sprout from the stem — remove all but one, which is grown-on to form a rod or single cordon. To grow a double cordon, leave one shoot either side of the main stem.

Prune the lateral or the laterals of the single and double cordon in mid summer by cutting them back to about 15 cm (6 in) from the main stem.

In winter, prune these laterals again to at least three buds. The leader should not be pruned in winter, except to remove the tip to encourage the development of side shoots.

Another popular espalier form is the dwarf bush pyramid. This consists of a centre stem with a number of branches extending outward. The bottom branches are usually about 45 cm (18 in) long, and each succeeding branch about 5 cm (2 in) shorter up to the top branches, which will end up as around 15 cm (6 in) in length. The result will be a dwarf, pyramid-shaped tree. All side shoots are pruned in the same way as the other cordons. No posts or wires are needed as the tree, although clipped into a neat geometric shape, will still be bushy enough to stand alone.

Trees are planted about 1 m (3 ft) apart so that when fully grown the basal branches of each tree will just touch that of its neighbour.

When growing cordons and espaliers, strong supports and shelter from strong winds and hard frosts are essential.

Like ordinary fruit bushes and trees, cordons are subject to the usual diseases, and winter and summer spraying may be necessary. (See Chapter 9, pages 126–139.) Gardeners will find that the cordon system is one of the best ways to grow fruit since the method requires minimal space and makes it easy to prune, pick and spray the crops.

Dwarf fruit trees rarely exceed 2–4 m (7–14 ft) in height but bear full-sized fruit. Like the one above, many varieties have space-saving upright columnar growth.

CHAPTER FOUR

Planting an edible garden

On the whole it's wiser to aim for a certain amount of formality in the basic planting design of your potager. In a design that is too informal, larger plants will need to be supported or they'll flop on top of other low-growing crops; it's easier to avoid this if the edibles are grown in more formal rows or clumps. Another problem is that harvesting produce can leave gaps that detract from the garden's appearance, so the overall design must be strong enough to disguise bare patches of soil until the next crop is sown. This is why experienced vegetable gardeners choose a symmetrically balanced design.

The basics
Achieving symmetry
Formal gardens are in vogue again as gardeners have come to realise that formality doesn't necessarily mean rigidity, that informal plantings are enhanced by strict linear confines and that symmetry itself is pleasing to the eye. This doesn't mean that each bed in the potager must be a mirror image of the others, which would be both boring and produce a glut of identical produce at the same time.

A pleasing balance in the planting scheme is achieved by choosing different plants with similar colours and heights rather than in using identical plants. For example, the feathery tops of carrots and the foliage of Japanese mustard look alike at a distance, as do parsnips and celery and other edibles.

Another fun way to achieve symmetry is by the careful placing of plants or structures to achieve vertical accents. Climbing plants on tepees,

This stunning ornamental edible garden is full of fun and dynamic design concepts. Vegetative support poles and seats of vibrant blue create a dramatic juxtaposition with bold flower colours and with the archway and framework of traditional woven willow.

standard rose bushes or rosemary, clipped bay trees, or containerised topiary specimens placed at identical intervals in each section of the potager will create a sense of unity and give an impression of symmetry, even if all the plants in the beds beneath are different.

The simplest design for achieving symmetry is a basic square or rectangle, divided into four parts by a wide central path and slightly narrower side paths. The wider path provides a strong axis in the traditional European style, and further emphasis may be obtained by using espaliered fruit trees, or a sequence of clipped box shapes to border these paths. The bigger the edible garden, the bigger the plants can be, which allows the division of each major part into its own smaller pattern.

Scale

As with all gardens, the most important aspect to consider in planning the potager is that of proportion and scale. As a basic principle, all the components of the design — the shape and size of the beds, the paths, the boundary hedges or walls — should be on the same scale. A small edible garden with high boundary enclosures will look cramped no matter how hard one works at planting plans. The same sized garden with low enclosures, narrow paths and small beds containing plants of compact growth habit will look neat and spacious.

Similarly, a large garden looks best with high enclosures, wide paths and big beds. Filling it with an elaborate pattern of small beds and complex paths will produce a fussy, claustrophobic effect. If you prefer small beds for ease of access and maintenance, it's wise to group them into block patterns which can be repeated in rhythmic composition round the rest of the garden.

An alternative method of incorporating small beds into a large-scale plan is to subdivide some of the larger beds with small pathways. This allows the growing of large crops such as brassicas, while the smaller beds accommodate more compact edibles — but care must be taken that these subdivided beds don't unbalance the unity of the overall design. The ground-plan layouts in Chapter One (see pages 18–21) illustrate that the best position for them is in the centre of the potager where they will balance each other, or in the centre of each big block of beds where they'll echo the pattern of the main block.

Plan your planting

Having read Chapter 1 and chosen your basic ground-plan design, you now need to consider the practicalities of actually growing the plants. If you try to put plants together which have different cultivation requirements, or which will be vastly disproportionate in size, there will be disasters, leaving glaring

and ugly gaps in the overall plan. Even with a simple design it's worth taking time to make a planting plan. Use coloured pencils, or devise a set of symbols to indicate size, colour and texture of the plants required, and start by marking in all the obvious viewing places. Add some dotted lines to indicate which areas can be seen from each of these places, but remember that the areas will alter as various plants reach maturity.

Allow optional plant choices. Flexibility and a supply of back-up plants will help you combat the worst vagaries of the weather, pests and diseases, and gaps left by harvesting. This last is especially important because the vast proportion of edibles are annuals, and in one short growing season there is no time to rectify mistakes! Edible plants, unlike shrubs and perennials, don't transplant well.

It's also wise to also make a rough plan for the next season's crop so you'll be able to see at a glance which vegetables you'll need to sow to replace

A great deal of planning at ground level has gone into this beautifully laid out and well-proportioned potager. Lavender-edged brick pathways create symmetrically appealing patterns and outline beds of varying geometric shapes.

Featuring different foliage forms, colours and textures, this ornamental edible garden offers a mosaic of colour and scent. Silvery onion spears topped with pom-pom flower heads contrast with red and green lettuce and a haze of blue borage. At the rear, old red and pink roses are underplanted with red bergamot, bronze fennel, red orache, vibrant red astilbes, scarlet sage, crimson rainbow beet and orange nasturtiums.

those you're harvesting. This will avoid large patches of bare earth and the resulting unwelcome drop in productivity. It will also help reduce glut — the culinary possibilities of a whole bed of cabbages maturing at once is limited and somewhat daunting to say the least. Seasonal planting plans are invaluable also for practising plant- and crop-rotation — the soil will soon become exhausted if the same crops are continually planted in the same area. (See advice on crop rotation, Chapter 9, page 128.)

If you have an informal edible garden consisting of one or a few large beds, or if your formal layout consists of a few basic shapes, planning the planting will be straightforward. If your ambitions have led you to an elaborate layout with multiple beds, it's wise to block them out on graph paper first to help you assess how many plants of each variety you'll need to fill each area. Remember to mark which area of the potager faces north (or south if you're in the Northern Hemisphere) — this is very important for deciding where to locate taller edibles and those which prefer either sun or shade.

Now the fun starts as you browse through nursery catalogues to plan what exciting edibles to try. Plan for maximum visual impact by deciding which vegetables will complement each other colour-wise, and remember to consider the height each will attain at maturity — it's boring playing hunt the (weak and spindly) radishes beneath the huge leaves of the broccoli.

Pick up your wooden pegs, string, bottles of sand, go forth, measure up and move on to framework construction in the next chapter.

All vegetables are beautiful, but it goes without saying that some are more beautiful than others! Each has its own shape, colour, texture, volume and taste; each evolves over a season into something very different from how it started out, whether that was as a plant purchased from a garden centre, or one grown from seed. In terms of garden design, growing vegetables is a little like 'foliage gardening', since the leaves of vegetables offer an infinite variety of shapes, textures and size, and generally occupy more space than their actual flowers or fruit. Flowers which aren't those of fruiting plants are grown in an edible garden as companion plants or aromatics, but the basic tapestry comes from foliage of different heights and textures, with ornamental veges strongly featured.

Colour, texture, shape & size

To the casual onlooker, vegetables just have green leaves and are uninteresting, but if asked to look more closely, they will observe an enormous range of shapes and textures and variations in all shades of green. Cabbages vary from pale smooth drumheads or ox hearts to dark, bluey-green, bubbly-leafed savoys. Broad beans stand tall with grey-green leaves and clusters of black and white scented flowers that turn into beautiful fat shiny pods. French beans make low mounds of almost heart-shaped mid-green leaves, while runner beans scramble vigorously up supports to flaunt flowers of vibrant coral red. Parsnips and carrots sprout delicate feathery plumes; onions and leeks thrust up spears of silvery blue; and block plantings of potatoes offer foliage of dark rich green with masses of white or purple flowers.

Creative combinations

A desire to experiment with both traditional and exciting new hybrid veggies is born out of an appreciation of both the beauty and productivity of edible plants as we come to realise that there is as much scope for experimenting with colour in the vegetable garden as there is in flower borders. The choices are endless, but you could consider any of the following:

- For a gentle blending of colour, try a row of butterhead lettuces with soft

How to cope with excess produce

The essential rule for storage is that, regardless of time of ripening, when harvested, fruit and vegetables must be in perfect condition. Resist the temptation to store bruised, damaged or unripe fruit. It will spoil, rot quickly and contaminate others in the batch. Bruised or damaged fruit need not be wasted. Cut out inedible bits and eat fresh, cook or freeze.

It is also essential that all fruit and vegetables are stored in a dry, cool, well-ventilated frost-free place. Frost will quickly destroy produce.

Regarded as a dietary staple for many centuries, the humble cabbage is humble no more. A block planting of winter savoy hybrids with magnificent silver-purple leaves are set off to perfection by clipped hedges of golden-tipped box and balls of privet.

green leaves unfolding from a paler heart, in juxtaposition with a row of stiff-leaved cabbages with purple-red veinings on bold silvery-blue leaves.

- A bed offering exciting contrast of foliage form, texture and colour might incorporate informal plantings of globe artichokes, frilly oak-leaved lettuces of red and green, and clumps of bush or dwarf beans with heart-shaped leaves and flowers of varying colours.

- A combination of bold colours could comprise rows of tagetes (marigolds) and modern hybrid beetroots with glossy green foliage, heavily tinged and veined with purplish-red.

- Gold and bronze climbing nasturtiums could scramble up a tepee of climbing beans with their bright coral flowers.

- Brilliant flowers such as dahlias (especially hybrids with stunning purple-black leaves) or zinnias provide visual excitement and contrast to the darker green of leafy vegetables.

- Experimenting with shades of silver can also be rewarding. The dramatic felted foliage of the globe artichoke and its relative, the cardoon, offer restful silver tones.

- For another striking variation of colour, form and texture, group artichokes or cardoons with white cosmos and border these with clumps

of cool blue lavenders — a planting combination that bees and beneficial insects find irresistible.

- Edible plants with variegated leaves also offer an opportunity to create contrast in the garden. These include some cucurbits with dark green foliage dappled with greyish-white, and herbs such as mint, marjoram and lemon balm.
- Variegated sages with light green foliage splashed gold (var. 'Icterina') are particularly attractive. Common sage (*Salvia officinalis*) comes with dark grey-green leaves flushed rosy-purple and there is a delightful variant (*Salvia officinalis* var. *purpurea*) bearing cream and green foliage with purple-pink overtones.
- Edible nasturtium cultivar 'Alaska' offers striking foliage marbled cream.
- Other vegetables, although not strictly variegated, have stems which are markedly different from their leaves. These include golden celery, the Chinese brassicas, kohlrabi (which comes in two colours — white stems with pale green leaves, or pink-flushed silvery foliage above rosy-purple stems and bulb), beetroot with reddish stems and deep green leaves veined wine-red and, of course, the glowing rainbow chards.
- The popular red bunching onion (*Allium fistulosum*) is an eye-catching plant.

Block plantings of potatoes, broccoli and broad beans offer variation of foliage colour, form and texture in this healthy and productive potager. The prolific, rich red rose 'Dublin Bay', underplanted with cucurbits and catmint, the white walls and striped blinds of the cottage combine to create an attractive and colourful setting for the vegetable beds.

This larger ornamental edible garden features a variety of vegetables. Edged with parsley, the front bed features beetroot, red lettuce and carrots and a deep border of the edible marigold *Calendula officinalis*, backed by parsley and nasturtiums. Beds to the left contain onions, spring onions and young dwarf beans. Those to the right, bordered by chives, feature rows of the handsome dark red beetroot 'Bulls Blood'.

Grown and used in the same way as spring onions, it has vibrant red stalks which add pizazz to salads and other dishes.

- A border of wine-red ruby chard backed by the silver spears of leeks is another combination offering dramatic juxtaposition of colour, texture and form.
- Other edible plants providing garnet-red tones include the amaranth species, rhubarb, rainbow chard, tall red orache, red Brussels sprouts, sweet and chilli peppers, tomatoes, yellow-flowered but purple-stemmed oriental mustard, radicchio, chicories, red cabbages, darker beetroots such as 'Bull's Blood', aromatic reddish-purple perilla and several basil cultivars.
- The choice of aesthetically pleasing red-tinged and green-bronze ornamental lettuces is extensive — some having oak-shaped or attractively ruffled leaves. They are ideal to use as border plants or quick fillers, or as colourful plants in association with vegetables of solid reds.

The key to successful colour permutations in the edible garden, however, is happy experimentation. A seed catalogue or the range available at any good nursery shows that the variety of exciting vegetables, fruit and herbs is greater

than ever before. Each might be on offer as a number of different cultivars —
a bonus which leads the vegetable gardener on a voyage of (edible) discovery!

See the Quick Reference Guide, Chapter 8, pages 118–125, for the life
cycle, size, colour and best siting of vegetables and fruit.

General management in the edible garden
Continuity of produce and catch crops

There are a number of ways to maximise yields and ensure a steady
continuity of produce.

1. Maintain a high state of soil fertility with regular dressings of compost,
   organic materials, organic plant foods and manure so that plants can be
   grown at the greatest density. Detailed information on fertilisers is given
   in Chapter 7, page 115.
2. Extend the growing season over prolonged periods by sowing early,
   middle and late varieties. Your nurseryman will recommend appropriate
   cultivars. If you don't have a greenhouse, build a basic cold frame (see
   Chapter 7, page 112). Fill it with pots of seedlings to replace plants once
   they have cropped. Harden the seedlings off in a sunny, sheltered corner
   before planting out. Protect early season seedlings with polythene cloches
   (Chapter 7, page1 111–112).
3. For sustained yields, make successive sowings of each vegetable rather
   than one main crop. Glut is fine if you've time for, and enjoy, freezing,
   jamming, juicing, saucing, pickling and puréeing. If the crops in your
   veggie garden all mature at once, your family may not appreciate becoming
   vegetarian slave labourers struggling to fill a dozen chest freezers!
4. Interplant larger, slow-to-mature vegetables with catch crops. 'Catch'
   crops are smaller, quick-to-mature vegetables such as salad-stuffs, oriental
   vegetables, dwarf beans, peppers and chillies etc., which may be planted
   under or between larger vegetables and utilised as 'fillers'. They maximise
   soil space and help prevent weed formation.

A to Z of Vegetables

The list of vegetable varieties that follows is by no means exhaustive but
noted are cultivars for which seeds or plants are obtainable from nurseries
throughout the United Kingdom, Europe, North America, Canada, New
Zealand and Australia, in areas where geographic location and climatic
conditions permit their cultivation. It's wise when purchasing plants to check
their suitability for your climatic region.

Chosen for good cropping, hardiness, and disease-resistance, the varieties
recommended include traditional stalwarts, modern hybrids, dwarf and
heirloom cultivars.

Storing fruit & vegetables

Be forearmed — knowing
how to store and preserve
your crops *before* you plant,
before everything seems to
be ripening at once, will avoid
wastage and allow your family
to enjoy eating favourite fruit
and vegetables in winter and
during the off-season months.
All crops should be harvested
at the peak of their season
when in their prime, but late-
to-mature fruits can be just
as good.

Storage methods

- Vegetables: Store in the
  ground, dry store, dry,
  freeze or preserve
- Fruit: Dry store, dry,
  bottle, freeze or preserve
- Herbs: Dry, freeze,
  preserve in oil or vinegar

Incredible edibles: reliable veggies & gourmet delights

Globe artichokes

● ARTICHOKES, Globe, *Cynara scolymus*

Originating in the Mediterranean, globe artichokes were considered a delicacy by the Greeks and Romans. Introduced into France in the sixteenth century, they spread rapidly around the world, reaching the United States with French and Spanish settlers around 1800. A highly ornamental plant, the globe artichoke is tall and statuesque, with generous, deeply dissected silver foliage. It is grown for its large and delicious flower head, which is harvested while still immature, before the scales begin to open. The flesh at the base of the scales is sweet and tender and considered a gourmet delight.

Plant artichokes out of doors in spring in a fairly rich, moist but well-drained soil. They're gross feeders and do best in well-manured soil. Mulch and water during summer to encourage large, succulent heads. Given a position in full sun, artichokes will adapt to cooler climates, but they need space — their dramatic silver leaves can span up to 1 m (3 ft) and their flower stalks reach up to 1.5 m (5 ft). Artichokes are easily raised from seed, one to a pot.

Preferred varieties
'Purple de Jesi': *Tender purple-tinged small heads.*
'Green Globe': *Large green heads.*
'Purple Globe' and 'French Purple': *Purple heads.*
'Imperial Star': *Good-sized heads in first season.*

● ARTICHOKES, Jerusalem, *Helianthus tuberosus*

This tall handsome plant is neither an artichoke nor from Jerusalem but a sunflower which forms plump tubers. Originating from North America, it requires hot summers to form its bold golden blooms, which follow the arc of the sun.

The plants reach 2.4 m (8 ft) in height and provide an excellent temporary screen or backdrop in the edible garden. They have hairy green leaves and tough stems and are a thirsty species.

Although Jerusalem artichokes will grow easily from the peelings of a previous crop, the crop yield depends on the size of the tuber planted. Pinch out flowers as this appears to encourage plants to form large tubers. The tubers have red or cream skin, with white flesh. Red-skinned varieties are less knobbly to peel and have a slightly better flavour. High in vitamin C, Jerusalem artichokes make a flavoursome potato replacement and can be eaten raw in salads, roasted, boiled and mashed.

Plant (preferably) full-sized tubers 30 cm (1 ft) apart in moist, fertile soil in early spring. It's best to uplift all tubers at harvest because they quickly reproduce to form a dense clump. Some frost tolerance.

Preferred varieties:
'Friseau': *large, easily peeled red tubers, smooth reddish skin.*
'Dwarf Sunray': *compact plant, long smooth-skinned tubers.*

Leafy Asian greens.

● ASIAN GREENS

Asian greens comprise a large group of versatile, quick-to-mature vegetables for salads and stir-fries. Small in size, they make excellent catch crops and container plants.

Sow small numbers of seeds at regular intervals, straight into enriched soil or pots for continuous cropping. Seedlings don't transplant well, so thin out, leaving only the strongest plants. Asian greens require regular watering, moist soil and sun/part shade to prevent bolting in hot, dry conditions.

Asian salad greens include leafy varieties such as 'Mizuna' and 'Mibuna', known as Chinese lettuce and Japanese greens. Pick a few leaves at a time for sustained cropping rather than harvesting the whole plant. Generally frost hardy.

Preferred varieties

Of the many Asian greens suitable for both eating raw in salads or for cooking, among the most popular are Chinese white cabbages.

'One Kilo' and 'Two Seasons': *Upright oval heads.*

Tat-soi, Bok Choy: *Dwarf upright cabbage, crisp white stems.*

Pak Choi: *Oriental broccoli, single-flowering green and purple heads.*

● ASIAN RADISH

Treasured for oriental cooking. Of the many varieties available, the Japanese and daikon radishes are popular. Larger and stronger-tasting than the European varieties, they're used raw in salads, in side dishes, cooked in stir-fries and soups, and steamed or braised whole.

Preferred varieties

'Radish Chinese Half Long Green': *Popular long-rooted Chinese radish with green skin and white tips.*

'Tokinashe': *Long-rooted, white-fleshed variety for year-round sowing in all but the coldest regions.*

'Aomaru Koshin': *Unusual large, round, flat-bottomed root, green skin and red-purple rays spreading through centre — a colourful salad vegetable when sliced.*

● ASPARAGUS (*Asparagus officinalis*)

The French philosopher and playwright Marcel Proust, overcome by the beauty of asparagus tips, describes his delight thus:

> *'A vegetable dipped in pink and ultramarine, spikes delicately daubed with mauve and azure changing colour little by little down to their feet . . . with iridescences that are not of this world . . .'* Art of French Vegetable Gardening, *Louisa Jones (full details in bibliography)*

He was doubtless aware that it was also exceptionally good to eat!

This southern European plant is a long-lived perennial cultivated for its rich succulent tips. Many gardeners are put off growing asparagus because it requires a permanent bed, takes two years to crop, and its fruiting season is brief. It is, however, a rewarding plant because it can remain in the same ground for years, and is highly decorative during summer and autumn when its strong green plumes gradually turn to butter-gold. (It looks marvellous with vibrant dark-coral nasturtiums.) A small bed gives great pleasure in spring when — like magic — the fat new tips appear. Keep the empty bed weed-free by over-sowing with a green manure cover crop (see page 131) such as phacelia, catch crops, salad greens or pot marigolds.

Asparagus requires a sunny, well-drained, moderately fertile soil. Start by buying one- or two-year-old crowns and plant 45 cm (18 in) apart in a well-prepared trench and wait until the second year before harvesting. Alternatively, sow all-male F1 hybrid seeds in pots before moving them into the prepared bed. These will yield a small harvest during the second summer. Well cared for and not over-cropped, this gourmet vegetable will produce ever-increasing shoots for 10 to 20 years — a fine reward for a little space!

Preferred varieties

'Lucullus': *Excellent cropper.*
'Franklin': *Thick meaty spears, crops heavily.*
'Sweet Purple': *Sweet thick purple spears.*
'Giant Mammoth': *Thick succulent spears.*
'Martha Washington': *Established favourite in the USA, crops heavily, rust-resistant.*
'Connover's Colossal': *Large tasty green spears.*

Asparagus

Aubergine/eggplant

● AUBERGINES/EGGPLANTS (*Solanum melongena*)

A beautiful tropical and subtropical vegetable grown in China and India for nearly 3000 years and brought to the New World by Moorish invaders.

The eggplant is a decorative vegetable, its glossy midnight-black fruit adding dramatic colour and accents among other crops. It is also attractive in bloom, bearing dark lilac-purple flowers; some varieties have purple stems.

A grouping of three varieties of mixed colours makes a stunning corner or centrepiece for a courtyard or container garden. Harvest aubergines when young and tender — they're excellent for frying, roasting, pickling and for many other culinary uses.

In colder zones, the plant requires greenhouse or container cultivation, but in temperate climates does well in any sunny, sheltered corner. The plant rarely exceeds 1 m (3 ft), with dwarf varieties, less. Pinch out main tips to encourage bushy growth. Many varieties of aubergines with whitish egg-shaped fruit exist but they're less prolific than the familiar polished purple-black varieties.

The plants and fruit of the Japanese hybrids are smaller, but mature earlier and yield abundantly, often bearing 40–50 fruit per stem.

Aubergines require a loose, well-drained soil, rich but slightly acidic, and consistently warm temperatures. Cultivars over 45-cm (18-in) tall need staking to support weight of fruit. Water well to avoid leaf- and bud-fall.

Beans

Preferred varieties

'Tokyo Black' and 'Japanese Long Tom': *Small fruit, mature early, crop heavily.*
'Black Beauty': *Old traditional favourite, suited to warmer climates, prolific, large teardrop-shaped purple-black fruit on bushy plant.*
'Early Long Purple': *Elongated deep violet fruit, quick to mature, hardy to cooler zones*
'Bonica F1': *Elongated fruit, cold-tolerant.*

Dwarf varieties

'Gourmet's Delight', 'Bambino',' Hestia'.
'Easter Egg': *Early cropping, oval-shaped white satin-skinned fruit. Excellent container specimen.*

Heirloom varieties

'Violetta de Firenze': *Internationally popular, highly decorative oblong to round fruits in shades of lavender-striped creamy-white. Crops heavily, tolerant of less than perfect conditions.*

● BEANS

Cultivated since earliest times, this versatile vegetable was brought to Europe by the Spanish in the sixteenth century. With decorative flowers and pods, beans come in a delightful range of colours, shapes and sizes, and some varieties have patterned skins.

Sow beans in pots in spring and plant out when warm weather is assured. Space bush beans 12–16 cm (5–6 in) apart in well-manured, moisture-retaining soil. Avoid nitrogenous fertilisers, which promote lush foliage at the expense of flowers. Beans are a valuable crop for fixing nitrogen in the soil.

Beans need constant harvesting for continual cropping. Plants are prone to black- and white-fly infestation, so repel pests by planting feverfew with early varieties and nasturtiums with late varieties.

Dwarf or bush beans (*Phaseolus vulgaris*)

Grown for small, tender beans, bush cultivars mature quickly, make good fillers and are perfect for small spaces and containers. Among the bush varieties, the yellow butter beans and the purple-podded varieties are both delicious and decorative.

Preferred varieties:

'Purple Tee Pee': *Stringless snap beans.*
'Long John': *Green stringless pods.*
'Gourmet Delight': *High-yielder, rust-resistant, suited to both hot and cold climates.*
'Canadian Wonder': *Green flat pods.*
'Purple Queen': *Attractive glossy almost stringless purple pods.*
'Bountiful Butter': *Tender yellow waxen pods.*
'Roquefort': *French heirloom, delicious golden pods, crops heavily.*

Runner or climbing beans (*P. multiflorus, P. coccineus*)

Among the most prolific and easily grown of vegetable crops. Grown on tepees of wooden or bamboo stakes, climbing beans make strong vertical accents in the edible garden and provide vivid colour with ornamental flowers ranging from deep scarlet, coral-red, lavender or white, depending on the variety.

Preferred varieties:
'Scarlet Runner': *Vibrant coral-red flowers, flattish full-flavoured green beans.*
'King of the Blues': *Attractive blue-black pods, some heat tolerance.*
'Blue Lake' and 'Broker': *Both heat-tolerant and yield heavily.*
'Painted Lady': *Decorative red and white flowers, long tender pods.*

● BROAD BEANS (*Vicia faba*)

Thought to have originated from the Mediterranean around 6500BC, broad beans are now popular worldwide.

Broad beans provide nourishing, protein-packed food and nutritious waste for composting. Nitrogen compounds made by bacteria in the roots and fixed in the soil are released to the next crop. In temperate climates, sow broad beans into the soil in late autumn to over-winter. In coldest areas, sow in pots indoors and plant out when soils are warmer.

The long-pod varieties, with 8–10 beans per pod, are tall — 1.2 m (3 ft 3 in) and need support. Pinch out tips at 1 m (3 ft) to prevent them becoming leggy, and to promote more flowers.

Preferred varieties
Long-pods
'Exhibition Longpod' and 'Sutton's Green': *Popular abundantly cropping stalwarts.*

Dwarf varieties
'Windsor': *Short pods, standard and dwarf form.*
'The Sutton': *Popular compact cultivar to 30 cm (1 ft) high.*
'Coles Dwarf', 'Coles Early Dwarf' and 'Dwarf Prolific': *1–1.5 m, abundant croppers.*

Heirloom varieties
'Aquadulce': *Long-podded, white-seeded cultivar.*
'Crimson Flowered': *Decorative and colourful flowers and fruit.*
Cultivation requirements are the same as for other bean varieties.

Broad beans

Beetroot

● BEETROOT (*Beta vulgaris*)

Grown since Assyrian times, the beetroot was highly revered by the ancient Greeks, and in Europe appears in recipes from 1558. Both standard and globe varieties come in many exciting colours and shapes, but the most decorative for the edible garden are the old-fashioned wine-red varieties.

These old-favourites have decorative rich green foliage tinged crimson above garnet globes; others have green leaves, pink stems and globes ringed with white. Newer varieties offer both white and gold fruit which don't 'bleed' and create an attractive contrast in both salads or cooked vegetable dishes.

Patient vegetables, beetroot can remain in the ground for some time before they get woody and past their prime. In all but the coldest months they make a beautiful combination mixed with dwarf nasturtiums or the silvery spears of leeks. Beetroot crops also make attractive borders.

Start beetroot in pots in early spring, or sow out of doors in early summer about 5 cm (2 in) apart. Seed won't germinate at temperatures lower than 7°C (45°F). Don't thin the seedlings, they'll push each other out of the way to form tender young baby beets. Beetroot require well-drained but moist, light soil with high nitrogen levels and plenty of humus, but no fresh manure.

In addition to the traditional globe-shapes, modern varieties also come with cylindrical, long flat or oval roots.

Preferred varieties
'Forono' and 'Cyndrica': *Cylindrical roots.*
'White': *Colourless flesh.*
'Egyptian': *Red flattened globe-shaped roots.*

Gourmet varieties
'Detroit Dark Red': *Large globes.*
'Burpees Golden Globe': *Non-bleeding, tasty yellow flesh.*
'Albino': *White globe.*
'Rapid Red' and 'Fuer Kugal': Can be sown year-round in temperate climates.

Heirloom varieties
'Chioggia': *Italian variety, sweet mild flavour.*
'Bull's Blood': *American heirloom, claret-tinged foliage, pink and white striped flesh.*

Dwarf varieties — mini beets
Baby beets are favourites for catch crops, containers or small beds. Their sweet-flavoured bite-sized miniature globes make them universally popular as gourmet baby vegetables.
Baby Beets: 'Mini Gourmet', 'Detroit Little Ball' and 'Tardel'.
With delightful bite-sized fruits, mini beets make excellent catch crops and container specimens.

● SILVERBEET — Swiss chard (*Beta vulgaris* var. *cicla*)

A colourful, versatile vegetable, silverbeet is both cold- and heat-hardy and can be grown almost year-round in all but the coldest climates. Silverbeet or Swiss chard is highly decorative and its vertical growth habit makes it an excellent small-space crop. The bright, translucent wine-red or golden stems glow in the sun, contrasting beautifully with the topping of dark green bubbly foliage, which is rich in vitamins, and used as a salad and spinach-type vegetable. Harvest stalks young on a cut-and-come-again principle. About 60 cm (2 ft) at maturity, rainbow beets make exciting colour contrasts in the edible garden and are so ornamental they're often grown in the flower bed, and not harvested at all!

Silverbeet will cope with container cultivation and diverse soils. Like beetroot, each 'seed' is a cluster of seeds and the weakest can be nipped out to leave the strongest seedlings. Water them regularly in hot, dry periods to prevent bolting.

Preferred varieties

'Tricolour': *Universally popular, with stems of gold, red and white.*
'Fordhook Giant' and 'Argentata': *Green leaves, white stems.*
'Charlotte': *Eye-catching scarlet ribs, maroon foliage.*
'Bright Yellow': *Gold ribs, green foliage.*
'Ruby Chard', 'Rainbow Chard', 'Tricolour' and 'Bright Lights': *Green foliage, and variations of yellow, gold, pink or crimson stems.*

● BROCCOLI (*Brassica oleracea* subvar. *Botrytis* var. *cymosa*)

Said to have originated in the eastern Mediterranean, broccoli spread from Italy to the rest of Europe around 1560 and reached North American in 1800. Hailed as a powerful antioxidant, the vegetable is rich in dietary fibre, iron and vitamins A and C. Modern broccoli cultivars are highly decorative. The spiral-coned lime-green heads of popular hybrid 'Romanesco', piled up like layers of tiny seashells, or the little red mushrooms of the purple, cut-and-come-again varieties are both a culinary and visual delight. The foliage of most broccoli is an attractive silvery-green with pale midribs. Planting early, mid- and late-season varieties will allow harvesting over long periods.

Purple-sprouting and white-sprouting varieties make large spreading plants up to 1 m (3 ft) tall. The plants take up to 45 weeks from sowing to maturity, but since much of this time is over winter, they earn their space as groundcover and for early cropping in spring.

Sow broccoli seeds directly into the soil, scatter in small clumps, or use dwarf cultivars as an underplanting beneath taller vegetables of vertical growth habit. For continuous yield, always pick the centre stem of a mature broccoli plant first to encourage side-heads to develop for continuous yield.

Preferred varieties
Calabrese broccoli

'Mercedes' and 'Corvet': *Traditional early varieties, abundant croppers.*
'Winter Harvest': *Excellent late-season variety.*

Silverbeet, or Swiss chard

Broccoli

Brussels sprouts

'White' or 'Purple Sprouting': *Late varieties, crop through winter and spring in all but coldest climates.*

Dwarf (excellent for containers and small gardens)
'Brocoletto Raab': *Matures 6–8 weeks, button-sized florets, grows to just 24 cm (8 in) — ideal catch crop.*
'Magic Dragon' and ' Magic Dwarf': *Compact, central-heading varieties.*

● BRUSSELS SPROUTS (*Brassica oleracea bullata* subvar. *gemmifera*)
Brussels sprouts are thought to have originated in Belgium in the early seventeenth century, spreading rapidly from then on throughout the rest of Europe. Tall elegant plants, sprouts take around 28–36 weeks to mature, depending on the variety, and stand between 45 cm (18 in) and 1 m (3 ft) in height.

Rows of tall slim Brussels sprouts take little space and provide extended cropping if a variety of seasonal cultivars are sown and harvested regularly. In windy positions, sprouts may need staking since they're susceptible to wind-rock. Cultivation requirements as for broccoli.

Preferred varieties
Red
The most decorative of the sprout family and perfect for the ornamental edible garden are the cultivars red 'Rubine' and 'Ruby'. The former is more compact than the green varieties and has a more refined flavour. 'Ruby' is an heirloom variety with burgundy-red sprouts and lavender-blue leaves. 'Red Island Improved' and 'Long Isa Improved' are also high-yielding older varieties.

Green
'Montgomery': *Good cropper.*
'Tighthead': *Modern variety, prolific cropper.*
'Drumtight: *Adaptable to wide range of climatic conditions.*

● CABBAGES (*Brassica oleracea* subvar. *capitata*)
Cabbages were cultivated from earliest times in the eastern Mediterranean and Asia Minor. Many varieties have been developed over the centuries. Heat-tolerant types were bred in southern Europe and hard-headed varieties were introduced by the Celts and Scandinavians. German literature records the cultivation of red varieties in the eleventh century.

The humble cabbage is humble no longer. This erstwhile dietary staple now ranks as a designer veg, coming in multiple colours, sizes and shapes. Leaves may be pale green and smooth or crinkly, dark blue-green, or vibrant garnet-reds which enliven the potager and add colour contrast among other vegetables throughout the year.

Savoy cabbages are dark green, with deeply puckered, bubbly leaves. Red cabbages are fairly smooth and a deep purplish-red colour with a beautiful bloom on both sides of the leaves. The rich colour of red cabbages is a perfect colour foil to the silvery crinkled leaves of the hearty savoys.

Young cabbages can be underplanted with catch crops such as radish, lettuce or spring onions, which mature quickly, or with flowering companion plants. Cabbages have long been grown in rows but have far greater visual impact if they are grown in blocks. An added advantage is that one can crop from around the outer edges, thus avoiding a snag-toothed gap when a head is removed from a row. This is important in a small edible garden where limited space allows groups of only four to six. Cabbages look particularly attractive edged with dwarf marigolds.

The average cabbage stands 37–45 cm (14–18 in) high and spreads to 45 cm (18 in). Cabbages harvested in the spring generally have conical or 'ox-heart' heads. They over-winter from mid-to-late summer sowing, taking 30–40 weeks to mature. Summer and winter cabbages are generally round-headed and smooth-leaved. Late autumn and winter varieties have darker colours and less smooth leaves but this category also includes the white cabbages used for coleslaw. Both take 20–35 weeks to mature.

Cabbages require much the same cultivation methods as broccoli and sprouts, but they need controlled watering during dry periods. A sudden drenching can cause the heads to split, leading to deterioration of the flesh. It's wise to stagger plantings of cabbage using early, mid- and late-season varieties to avoid them all maturing at once. Wider spacing between cabbages produces bigger heads, but picked younger and smaller, their taste is much sweeter.

Preferred varieties
'Tundra': *Hardy red traditional variety, hardy to harsh winters.*
'Ruby Ball': *Stunning red cabbage for winter colour.*
'Rookie': *Universally popular deep-red cabbage, mature head weighing some 2 kg (4½ lbs).*

Heirloom variety
'January King': *Survives harshest of winters.*

Dwarf varieties:
'Mini', 'Copenhagen Market', 'Space Saver'.

Red varieties
'Purple Head', 'Hardora', 'Mammoth Red Rock'.

Green varieties
'Savoy', 'Hawke', 'Green Gold' (winter variety).

Cabbages

Chinese cabbages (*Brassica rapa* subvar. *pekinensis* and *chinenses*)
The flavour of versatile oriental cabbage hybrids is more delicate than that of traditional European varieties.

Their leaves are crisper and mature more quickly. Picked young, shredded finely and tossed in ginger, soy sauce, sesame seed and a little rice wine vinegar, they make deliciously crunchy stir-fries, salads or coleslaws. Most varieties can be sown almost year-round in temperate regions. The plants grow erect in warm temperatures but show a more prostrate habit in cooler conditions where they are remarkably cold-hardy.

Chinese cabbages come in many decorative and delicious forms. The traditional 'Two Seasons' variety crops from both early spring and summer–autumn sowings. A productive crop, it takes little space, having large oval heads 25 x 18 cm (9 x 7 in) with thick succulent midribs and crisp, tender, tightly furled savoy-type leaves.

Many other excellent Chinese greens are available. (Please see Quick Reference Guide, Chapter 8, Table 6, page 125, for a list of other hybrids and oriental vegetables.)

● CARROTS (*Daucus carota*)

Cultivated since earliest times around the Mediterranean and Asia Minor, carrots reached Europe in the twelfth century. The Pilgrim Fathers took the vegetable to North America where it was grown by early colonists in Virginia in 1609.

Carrots contain beta-carotene, Vitamin A, which helps ward off heart attacks and strokes, and discourages the formation of artery-clogging cholesterol.

Freshly dug carrots.

Carrots interplant well with onions and leeks — which gives protection from carrot fly. A row of mature carrots forms a stream of delicate fern-like foliage that makes a beautiful border and an excellent foil to the bolder foliage of brassicas and cucurbits.

Carrot seed is slow to germinate and requires stone-free, loose, free-draining soil with low nitrogen levels. Except for the round-rooted varieties, carrots are best sown straight into the soil.

In addition to the ubiquitous orange carrot, modern hybrids come with white, yellow, purple and violet fruits, some with rounded globes instead of elongated roots. Varieties to really colour your cuisine!

Preferred varieties
'Rondo': *Round roots, early traditional variety.*
'Nantes': *Mid season.*
'Berlicum-Berjo': *Late, prolonged cropping season.*

Dwarf varieties
'Mini Sweet', Paris Market', 'Amsterdam Forcing' and 'French Round', all with flavoursome miniature globe-shaped roots — favourites with restaurants and gourmet gardeners as 'baby vegetables'.

Heirloom varieties
'Purple Dragon': *Nutty-flavoured purple flesh.*
'Lubyana' and 'Yellow Austrian': *Yellow flesh.*
'White Belgium': *White flesh.*
'Nutri-red': *Coral flesh.*

● CAPSICUMS & CHILLI PEPPERS (*Capsicum annum*)

Chilli and sweet pepper plants originated from Central America and Mexico and were cultivated extensively by the Aztecs.

The colourful fruit grows on bushes to 1.2 m (3 ft 3 in) tall, depending on variety. Versatile, decorative plants, their abundant fruits are treasured for their pungent, aromatic flavours. Capsicum and chilli peppers come in myriad colours, sizes and shapes and in addition to their aesthetic appeal, their popularity in cuisine has resulted in the hybridisation of many new varieties of both. Many people believe peppers make food so hot that all other flavour is obliterated — an incorrect perception since many hybrids are sweet and juicy and have no heat at all.

However, hot chilli peppers carry oils called capsains which burn skin, so wash your hands well after handling seeds or plants, and avoid touching your eyes or nose. To skin chilli peppers painlessly, place under a preheated grill and turn frequently until skins are blistered and peel off. Chilli peppers dry well for prolonged storage.

Peppers mostly have small white blossoms and many varieties start green and ripen to their final colour. Sweet pepper hybrids come in red, purple, orange, green, yellow or gold. Modern introductions include 'tomato peppers' — borne on medium-sized bushes bearing prolific crops of thick-walled, juicy fruit — delicious cooked or raw. Most chilli varieties also ripen from green to red, and fruit vary from long and thin to short and fat.

Chilli and sweet peppers need a warm, sunny, sheltered spot in full sun and fertile, free-draining soil. F1 hybrids are available for cooler climates with shorter summers. Peppers have a small root ball and are best sown first in peat pots so that they can be transplanted without root disturbance when the soil is consistently warm. Plants may need staking to support weight of abundant fruit.

Dwarf varieties make eye-catching container subjects and add colour and visual appeal to the edible garden. In colder climates, containerised peppers can be moved into sheltered positions when required.

Preferred varieties
Bell and sweet peppers

Popular sweet varieties with thick-walled green fruits about 12 cm (5 in) long which redden as they mature. Their crisp texture makes them delicious for stuffing, frying or eating raw. Plants reach 60 cm (2 ft) high. International favourites include the prolific cropping

Gold: 'Golden California Wonder'.
Red: 'Cabernet', 'Marconi Red'.
Orange: 'Orange Sun'.
Yellow: 'Yellow Banana'.
Green: 'California Wonder'.
Purple: 'Purple Beauty'.

Bell peppers

Capsicums

Chilli peppers

Hot favourites
'Habanero Red', 'Asian Fire', 'Tabasco', 'Serrano', 'Jalapeno'.
'Rocoto Manzano' is cold hardy, fruits in winter in temperate regions.

Medium
'Anaheim', 'Cayenne', 'Black Hungarian' (heirloom).

Sweet/spicy
'Poblano', 'Mulato', 'Numex Sweet'.

Dwarf
'Orange Thai': Hot, finger-sized fruit, good fresh and dried.
'Pepper Sweet Pickle': Red, orange or yellow fruit on
one plant.

● CARDOON (*Cynara cardunculus*)

This handsome architectural Mediterranean native is valued in the
edible garden for both its aesthetic and culinary benefits. Cultivated
since ancient times, the cardoon reached Europe in 1658, and North
America in the 1700s.

A tall plant growing some 2 m (7 ft) high, the cardoon has giant,
deeply dissected silvery-green leaves, and spectacular lavender thistle-
like flowers.

The plant's thick white stalks are blanched and eaten in sauces, or like
celery, and the globular heads, cooked like those of the globe artichoke.
The cardoon is a perennial and reproduces itself by both offshoots and
seeds. The traditional variety, 'White Ivory', is the best edible hybrid.

Sow seeds in pots and plant outside in late spring, allowing 1 m (3 ft)
spacing between plants. Dress with manure or compost in winter and
don't allow cardoons to flower if you want to blanch the stems for eating.

● CAULIFLOWER (*Brassica oleracea* subvar. *botrytis*)

Of eastern-Mediterranean origin, cauliflowers were cultivated as early as the
sixth century BC and appeared in Europe by 1500.

Cauliflowers come in all-seasons varieties so plant early, mid- and late-maturing
plants for year-round supply. Generally a cold climate vegetable, choose a variety
with some heat tolerance for cultivation in warmer climates. Modern summer
varieties take about 20 weeks to mature and winter varieties 40–50 weeks.
Cauliflowers, like cabbages, look best grown in blocks so that harvesting can take
place from the outer edges, thus avoiding an empty gap in the middle of a row.

Space cauliflower plants in groups a minimum of 60 cm (2 ft) apart — they
mature to big vegetables. They require fertile soil and regular watering to prevent
bolting. Winter varieties benefit from dressings of compost or blood, fish and
bone meal. Like other brassicas, cauliflowers suffer from clubroot disease, so
crops need to be strictly rotated to avoid a build-up of disease spores in the soil.

Preferred varieties

The traditional creamy-white-headed varieties, though attractive in themselves, are now rivalled by hybrids with purple or lime-green florets. Exciting modern cultivars produced by the surprise marriage of the broccoli and the cauliflower are the delightful 'broccoflower' hybrids. These unique open-pollinated combinations prefer the cool, even-growing conditions of spring or autumn.

'Alverda', and 'Green Macerata': *combine the flavour of both parents.*

Purple-violet varieties

Easily grown, these varieties lose some colour on cooking, but the florets lend attractive accents and contrasts to salads and other cold dishes.

'Violet Queen': *Traditional purple variety, rich rosy-violet finely textured florets with high mineral content.*

'Violet Sicilian': *Purple florets.*

Orange variety

'Orange Bouquet': *Buttery orange head, high nutritional content.*

White varieties

'All Year Hybrid': *Early, prolonged cropping.*

'Phenomenal Early' and 'Snowball': *Heat tolerant for warmer zones.*

Dwarf varieties

Universally available, these dwarf white cauliflower hybrids make perfect container and small garden specimens. They also look marvellous whole on the dinner plate.

'Alpha' (syn. 'Polaris') 'Idol' and 'Snowball' (tennis-ball-sized heads).

Cauliflower

- CELERIAC (*Apium graveolens* var. *rapaceum*)

Celeriac, a European native and a relative of celery, is cultivated for the bulb at the base of its stem rather than for its stalks, which aren't considered edible. The bulb is delicious either grated raw in salads, or cooked. Celeriac makes a bushy plant about 45 cm (18 in) high, with celery-like dark green leaves. Space young plants 30 cm (1 ft) apart and remove lower leaves regularly to encourage the bulb to mature.

Grown in both cool and warm zones as an annual, celeriac requires a moist, enriched soil and regular watering in summer. Sow seed indoors in late winter and plant out in mid-spring.

Preferred varieties

'Snow White', 'Alabaster', 'Giant Prague' and 'Tellus': *Popular flavoursome bulbs.*

Celery

● CELERY (*Apium graveolens*)

Native to Europe and Asia, the best celeries for the edible garden are the modern, hardy, self-blanching and stringless American varieties — they don't need the soil 'earthed up' around them to give crisp white stalks.

Celery is a cool-weather crop requiring a long growing season. It likes a sunny position in moist, well-manured soil. Water regularly in dry weather to prevent premature seeding. Enjoy continuous cropping by picking the outer stalks and leaving the inner to grow-on.

Preferred varieties
Self-blanching American varieties include:
'Tall Utah': *Glossy dark green stems.*
'Green Crunch': *Stringless, good flavour, crisp texture.*
'Stringless American': *Green stems.*
'Celebrity': *Long crisp stems, some frost tolerance.*

Dwarf varieties
Ideal varieties for containers and the small edible garden include:
'Golden Self-Blanching': *Compact, pale golden leaves, thick stringless stems,
    disease-resistant, matures 11–17 weeks.*
'Crisp and Crunchy': *Compact cultivar to 32 cm (1 ft).*
'Ventura': *Heavy cropping, some disease resistance, suits a broad of range
    climatic conditions.*

Chinese celeries
The 'Kunn Choi' varieties are similar in form to traditional celery but differ in size, are stonger-flavoured, and quick to mature. With roundish stalks, plants reach 1.5 cm (½ in) in diameter and around 23 cm (9 in) in height. In colder zones, plants may be grown in pots outdoors for year-round supply. Sow seeds thickly, direct into the soil or a container, approximately 6 mm (⅛ in) deep and transplant when 10–12 cm (4–5 in) high to around 30 cm (1 ft) apart.

● CHICORY (*Cichorium intybus*)

A native of Europe spreading through to central Russia and western Asia, chicory has been cultivated for centuries for both culinary and medicinal purposes. The long-rooted varieties have also been used as a coffee substitute.

Both chicory and endive (see page 70) resemble lettuce and are used in salads. Endive has a loose heart — chicory has larger leaves and a compact heart. To remove its bitter taste, chicory is blanched by covering with pots, straw or black polythene for two to three weeks before harvesting. It is then called witloof.

Highly popular, the ornamental cabbage-shaped red radicchio chicory hybrids mature to give winter colour and don't require blanching. Chicory and endive hybrids are eye-catching border plants, and the green varieties, if allowed to seed, bear striking daisy flowers of intense blue. Other ornamental varieties come with intriguing green foliage splashed with red, or red stroked with white. Chicory is best suited to cooler climates.

Chicories and endives are best grown like lettuce in sun/part shade. Soils should be friable, moist and moderately rich. Plant green varieties in early summer and red varieties in mid to late summer and water well.

Preferred varieties
Red: 'Palla Rossa', 'Red Treviso Early' and 'Red Heart'.
Green: 'Sugarloaf', Crystal Heart' and 'Greenlof': *Self-blanching, lettuce-like heads, blanched hearts.*

● THE CUCURBIT CLAN: cucumbers, marrows, melons, pumpkins and squashes (courgettes/zucchini)

Originating from the Americas and cultivated for some 5000–10,000 years, the fruit and foliage of the extensive cucurbit family is among the most prolific and highly decorative of all vegetables.

The family includes cucumbers, squash (courgettes or zucchini), pumpkin and melons which crop from mid summer to late autumn. Their large bold foliage covers a considerable area, but cucurbits look marvellous when grown vertically on trellises, frames or archways. The hanging fruit, viewed at eye level instead of hidden beneath large leaves, makes a delightfully bold and decorative feature in the edible garden.

Another attractive idea, particularly in the small garden, is to plant cucurbits in large terracotta pots placed at intervals on top of a medium-height wall (for easy watering). The stems bearing fruit and golden chalice-shaped flowers make a superb focal point at eye level and leave the ground free for vegetables of a more terrestrial nature. Expose the developing fruits to the sun by removing old foliage. If crops are being grown at ground level, lift the developing fruits onto old bricks, tiles or flat stones.

Cucurbit flowers, ranging from pale lemon to deep gold, make eye-catching garnishes. For real flower power, if you've time (and patience), pull off a gourmet coup — serve the flowers filled with a delicate stuffing.

Despite their different names, summer and winter squash, pumpkins, cucumbers, marrows and courgettes/zucchini are warm-season crops but adaptable to most climates. They require a sunny position in moist, heavily composted and manured soil.

A nitrogenous fertiliser applied as flowers form promotes prolific crops. Seeds may be sown directly into mounded soil in summer. Water any of these types of squash regularly and pick fruit frequently for tenderness and continuous cropping. Pumpkin, which matures in autumn, may be stored for many months in a cool, dark place.

Summer squash

Courgettes

Cucumbers

Courgettes/zucchini (*Cucurbita pepo ovifera*)

Courgettes or zucchini, often referred to as squash, are baby bush marrows, bred for tender skin, good flavour and prolific cropping. They come in multiple colours, sizes and shapes and are outstanding ornamental fruits.

Spreading up to 1.2 m (3 ft 3 in) wide and growing 1 m (3 ft) tall, courgettes make handsome plants with silver-green, deeply cut leaves on prickly stems. Large golden chalice-shaped flowers turn into shiny fruit with dark or mid-green, golden yellow or almost white skin.

Golden-fruited courgettes are particularly attractive since they also have yellowish leaves, which brighten darker corners. Those with a flattened shape and scalloped edges are called scallopini.

Preferred varieties
Dwarf varieties
'Black Beauty', 'Costata Romanesco' and 'Blackjack': *Compact form, heavy croppers.*
'Greyzini': *Fruits have grey-green mottled skin.*
'Ambassador': *Prolific crops of dark green fruit, prolonged season, attractive container and small garden specimen.*

Standard varieties
'Golden' and 'Gold Rush': *Attractive bright yellow flavoursome fruits, mature quickly.*
'Golden Zucchini': *Golden fruit, decorative yellow foliage.*
'Burpee Golden Zucchini': *Small elongated yellow fruits.*
'Lebanese': *Heavy crops, tear-shaped green fruit.*

Summer squash
Both these cultivars are ideal for containers and small gardens.
'Green Button Hybrid': *Button squash, attractive scalloped lime-green fruit.*
'White Patty Pan': *Unusual flattened shape with scalloped edge.*

Cucumbers

Cucumbers are an indispensable salad vegetable. They require a warm, sheltered position in lightly limed soil. When watering, keep fruit and foliage dry to prevent mildew and fungal diseases. For heavier crops, dress with nitrogenous fertiliser when flowering begins. Pinch out tips when plant has made 7 leaves to encourage lateral shoots. Sow seeds indoors in spring; plant out in early summer. Frost-tender.

Preferred varieties
'Chinese Long Green', 'Long Green Ridge': *Prolific croppers.*
'Tasty Queen' and 'Diva': *Both seedless and mildew-resistant.*
'Burpless': *Non-bitter skin, low-acid flesh.*

Lebanese varieties
Small-growing cucumbers popular for delicate, slightly sweet flesh.

Apple cucumbers
Generally small and rounded in shape.
'Lemon': *Popular old favourite, prolific, burpless.*
'Crystal Apple': *Crunchy, sweet, prolific fruit*

Dwarf apple cucumber
'Spacemaster', 'Salad Bush', and 'Fanfare'.

Marrows
Fruit is allowed to grow bigger than zucchini but still requires harvesting while young and tender.

Preferred varieties
Most marrows are alike in flavour so with aesthetic appeal in mind, traditional
varieties might include:
'Long Green Striped': *Striped green and yellow.*
'Table Dainty': *Smaller, sweeter, golden-green colouration.*
'Long Green Bush' and 'Long White Bush': *Popular, prolific cropping.*

Pumpkins
One of the most attractive sights in the edible garden is pumpkin ripening in the golden autumn sun. Available in a diverse and fascinating range of colours, sizes and shapes, pumpkin and squash hybrids are bred for their dense, nutty-flavoured flesh, long storage life and decorative appearance. Their aesthetic appeal is so valued in Asian countries that they're used as ornaments or incorporated into floral and art displays before being eaten. A versatile vegetable, pumpkin can be grated raw into salads, cooked as soup, purée or soufflé, roasted, included in pickles, fried plain in fritters, used in cakes and pies, and even prepared as ice cream and jam.

Butternut pumpkin

Preferred varieties
'Sunburst': *Golden custard variety, round and flat
with beautifully scalloped edges.*
'Vegetable Spaghetti': *Flavoursome golden rugby-
ball-shaped fruit, prolonged storage.*
'Butternut': *Universal favourite, pear-shaped fruit,
creamy-orange in colour.*

'Hubbard' varieties
Other colourful hybrids to brighten the edible
garden in winter include:
'Golden Hubbard': *Rich gold colour.*
'Red Hubbard': *Vibrant coral-red.*

Ornamental cultivars
'Turk's Turban': *Pinkish-orange, striped green and
white. A protruding top makes it resemble an
elaborate turban.*

Dwarf varieties
Dwarf varieties suited to container cultivation and small gardens include:
'Golden Nugget' and 'Golden Buttons': *Pleasant nutty flavour.*
'Crown Prince' and 'Peek-A-Boo': *Bush varieties, small late fruit*
'Baby Bear': *Small orange fruit.*
'Jack-Be-Little' and 'Wee-Be-Little': *Tennis ball-sized fruit. Make intriguing individual vegetables on the dinner plate.*

● ENDIVE (*Cichorium endivia*)
Cultivated since ancient times, endive found its way from Egypt into Europe around 1548. A close cousin of chicory (see page 66) and cultivated in the same way, endive comes in two forms — broad-leaved, which looks much like a loose-leaf lettuce, and the bright light-green curly-leafed type, which provides exciting textural contrast in the garden.

Preferred varieties
'Green Curled': *Decorative deeply indented curly leaves, thick tender crisp ribs.*
'Italian Fine Curled': *Finely curled green leaves.*
'Pink Stem': *Attractive pinkish-green curly leaves.*
'Tres Fine Maraichere': *French gourmet delight, finely cut lacy leaves with crisp ribs and creamy heart.*
'Broadleaf Fullheart' (Batavian): *Frost-tolerant winter variety for colder climates.*

Pumpkin

Fennel

● FENNEL, Florence or Florentine (finnochio) (*Foeniculum vulgare* var. *azoricum*)
Treasured by the Greeks and Romans and cultivated for many centuries, Florence

fennel is rich in vitamins and both versatile and beautiful. Although closely related to the perennial herb fennel, this variety is grown as an annual for its bulbous leaf base, which has the texture of tender aniseed-flavoured celery. The bulb is partly visible above the soil. All parts of the vegetable are edible, including the seeds.

Standing about 45 cm (18 in) high, the plant has a fan of delicate fern-like light-green foliage similar to that of dill. Florence fennel, or finnochio, should not be confused with common fennel — the perennial grown as a herb for its richly redolent stalks and seeds, and sometimes purely for its highly decorative tall stems with filmy reddish-bronze plumes.

Preferred varieties
'Zefa Selmo Fina': *Some heat tolerance, thrives in hotter regions.*
'Zefa Tardo': *Thrives in cooler zones.*
'Leone': *Late variety, large white bulbs.*
'Dulce': *Sweet fennel, delicately flavoured tender flesh.*

● GARLIC (*Allium sativum*)

Cultivated since ancient times, garlic has multiple culinary uses, natural antiseptic properties, and is used as a companion plant to repel undesirable insects and to make non-toxic pesticides.

This indispensable herb has onion-like foliage and the base forms a series of small plump bulblets/cloves. Garlic is planted as an annual by detaching bulblets from the parent clove and requires a position of full sun and well-drained soil.

Preferred varieties

Of the many varieties of garlic, popular, well-tried and tested varieties include:
Chinese garlic: *Strong flavour.*
Elephant garlic: *Large juicy cloves, mild flavour.*
Italian garlic: *Red-skinned, easily peeled, rich medium flavour. Cultivar 'Printanor' has large mild-tasting cloves.*
Australian garlic: *'Oz Garlic Rosea'. Suited to hot climates and 'Oz Garlic White', suited to cooler climates. Both give 12–15 cloves per plant.*

Heirloom varieties

Specialist nurseries offer flavoursome heirloom varieties such as 'Rosa di Saluggia'.

Beds in front of this productive cottage garden potager are planted with a wealth of vegetables including broad beans, red and green lettuce, onions, red cabbage, kale, sage and other herbs. Companion plantings of flowers attract beneficial insects which encourage high pollination rates throughout the garden.

● KALE (*Brassica oleracea* var. *acephala*)

Grown since Roman times, this hitherto despised edible (often fed to sheep and cattle) has reached the ranks of designer veg. Extremely versatile, modern kales with their nuances of red, green, cream, pink and purple are among the most dramatic of all ornamental vegetables, treasured during winter months for their cheerful and extravagant colour combinations.

Low-growing and compact, they're particularly effective as container specimens, in block plantings and as temporary borders where their froths of pink, purple and cream among the green are inherently strong in structure and subtle in colour.

Kales vary in height from dwarf types about 30–40 cm (approx. 1 ft) high to tall varieties growing to 1 m (3 ft) and spreading to 60 cm (2 ft).

Pick kale leaves young and tender for both salads and cooked dishes. For the latter, the leaves are delicious sprinkled with a little soy sauce and fresh crushed ginger and lightly steamed. Use older leaves for decorative purposes — they make stunning 'plates' for salads, cold meats, fish, cheeses and other dishes. Harvest leaves of curly-leafed kales a few at a time for prolonged cropping.

A winter vegetable, kales have the same cultivation requirements as the brassica family (see pages 59–62).

Curly-leafed kale.

Kohlrabi

Preferred varieties
'Winterbore': *Vigorous F1 hybrid, cold-tolerant, abundant ruffled leaves, good raw or cooked.*
'Red Russian: *Siberian heirloom, wavy sweetly tender leaves, blue-green in temperate zones turning attractive purple-red in colder regions.*
'Ragged Jack': *Both cold- and heat-tolerant.*

Dwarf varieties
'Dwarf Green Curled': *Curly dark blue-green leaves.*
'Scotch' and 'Half Tall Scotch': *Tightly curled dark green leaves, extended cropping period.*

Ornamental kales
Colourful mixes include:
'Red Peacock' and 'White Peacock': *Dwarf feathery leaves.*
'Coral Queen': *Finely serrated coral-pink leaves surrounded by dark green outer leaves.*
'Red Bore F1': *Edible tightly frilled burgundy-purple leaves.*
'Tuscan Black': *Heirloom variety, large flavoursome ornamental leaves.*

● KOHLRABI (*Brassica oleracea* var. *gongylodes*)
An ancient vegetable, kohlrabi is grown for the swollen bulb-like base of its stem. White-stemmed with light green leaves and a white bulb, or purple-stemmed with purple-tinged leaves and a purple bulb, kohlrabi make amusing little plants which resemble sputniks. They provide an attractive edging for a bed of cabbages, either in the same colour or as a foil to different colours. Quick to mature, the bulbs, if harvested young, have a delicate nutty flavour and can be steamed or roasted and added to stir-fries and soups. Chopped finely, they make a colourful and unusual raw additions to salads.

Kohlrabi have the same cultivation requirements as brassicas (see pages 59–62).

Preferred varieties
'Purple Vienna': *Traditional variety, purple flattened globe-like bulb. Suitable late sowing/winter harvesting.*
'White Vienna': *Pale green skin, delicate white flesh.*
'Gigante': *Large bulbs with crisp white flesh.*

● KUMARA/SWEET POTATOES
Originating from ancient Peru, the sweet potato is now grown worldwide in temperate climates. The vegetable reached the southern hemisphere by 1400, and arrived in America and Europe around 1648. Sweet potatoes grow from a vine and require light, sandy soils.

Propagate by burying a mature tuber in a warm place in light, damp soil. When shoots form, uplift the tuber and divide it into pieces, ensuring that there is a shoot attached to each piece to form a new plant; and then replant.

Preferred varieties

Many sweet potato varieties exist worldwide but those popular for the home garden include 'Centennial' with bright copper-orange skin, and 'Jewel', a vigorous prolific variety with moist orange flesh.

Mature tubers are available in nurseries and supermarkets in orange, white, dark-red and yellow varieties. Although often unnamed, they're perfectly suitable for planting in the vegetable garden.

● LEEKS (*Allium porrum*)

Records dating back to 3200BC tell of leeks growing in ancient Egypt. A cold-hardy traditional winter vegetable with a fine, mild onion flavour, some varieties have decorative violet-blue upright spears that serve as an elegant foil for looser-leafed crops.

Leeks are easily germinated from seed and though they require garden space over several months, their striking vertical stalks add strength to the overall potager design. They can be interplanted with catch crops such as salad stuffs, beetroot or borders of flowers. Leeks, like onions, are often interplanted with carrots for mutual protection against insects and to utilise all available ground space.

The vegetable requires well-drained, rich, loose soil — essential if you intend to earth up soil around the white stems to blanch them. An alternative is to sow the seeds thickly and blanch by mulching deeply with compost as the plants grow.

Preferred varieties

'Mammoth Blanche': *Tall, thick-stemmed.*
'St Victor': *Flavoursome blue-leafed French hybrid.*
'Winter Giant': *Traditional heirloom variety.*
'Carentan Giant': *European heirloom variety, both cold- and wet-hardy,*
'Welsh Wonder': *Traditional popular variety.*

● LETTUCES (*Lactuca sativa*)

The days of the limp lettuce leaf are long gone. Modern lettuces are now among the most decorative of garden vegetables and are often used in the edible garden as edgers and left to grow tall and run to seed, or employed as alternating blocks of colour to give a patchwork and chequered effect. Modern hybrids come in multiple sizes, shapes and colours and all-seasons varieties. Leaf shape and texture are diverse.

Modern hybrids have been bred for cut-and-come-again cropping. One plant will give sustained yield if the leaves are frequently harvested.

With careful timing and selected varieties it's possible in all but the coldest zones to have lettuce year-round. They require a sunny position in compost and manure-enriched soil and frequent watering in warmer months to prevent bolting. Sow seed indoors in spring and transplant seedlings into soil in summer when about 5 cm (2 ins) high. Sow small amounts of seed regularly to avoid glut and for continuous cropping. Fortnightly applications of a nitrogenous liquid will ensure sweet, tender leaves.

Freshly dug leeks.

Cos lettuce and frilly 'Lollo Rosso'.

Lettuces come in a variety of shapes and colour.

Watermelon

Preferred varieties
Exciting international varieties include:
Red varieties
'Lollo Rosso', 'Casablanca', 'New Red Fire', 'Red Sails', 'Salad Bowl', 'Lovina', 'Merveille de Quatre Saisons' (all-seasons cultivar, cold-hardy) and 'Rouge d'Hiver' (cold-weather variety).

Green varieties
'Green Ice', 'Royal Oak Leaf': *Rich dark leaves.*
'Tango': *Deeply cut, pointed, endive-type leaves.*
'Lollo Biondo': *Ruffled leaves.*
Butterhead — 'Buttercrunch': *Soft smooth pale green foliage.*
Round-headed — 'Ice King' and 'Iceberg': *Large crisp round-headed varieties.*
Cos — 'Paris White': *Fine Cos variety.*

Dwarf varieties
'Mini Cos' and 'Little Gem': *Popular semi-Cos/Butterhead varieties, small sweet leaves.*
'Tom Thumb': *Miniature variety, small tender leaves.*

● MELONS (*Cucurbitaceae* spp.)
A member of the cucurbit family and an attractive and treasured summer fruit, melons come in many sizes, shapes and colours. Most fall into four main groups.
1. Rockmelon or cantaloupe: Broadly ribbed, warty skin and sweet orange flesh.
2. Honeydew: Light yellow-green skin and juicy green flesh.
3. Galia melons: An Israeli strain popular in Europe; round with greenish-yellow skin turning to gold.
4. Watermelons: Larger fruits with pale to dark striped skin, crisp red juicy flesh — seedless varieties are available.

Melons require moist, compost-enriched soil and controlled, plentiful watering during hot, dry periods. Sudden drenching causes skin to split and flesh to spoil. Keep fruit and foliage dry when watering to avoid mildew and fungal diseases. Sow seeds directly into the soil from late spring to early summer.

Preferred varieties
Rockmelon/cantaloupe
'Honeydew Green': *Pale green flesh, delicate flavour.*
'French Charantais': *Small orange flavoursome fruit.*
'Yellow Canary': *Golden-skinned, light green sweet flesh.*
'Tropical F1': *Green skin, yellow flesh, matures early. Suited to regions with short summers.*

Honeydew
'Honey Melon', 'Greenflesh', and 'Dewfresh': *Sweet juicy flesh.*

Watermelon
'Candy Red', 'Rapid Red': *Quick maturing, crisp fruit.*
'Sugar Baby': *Small round almost seedless fruit.*

● ONIONS (*Allium cepa*)

A vegetable of antiquity, onions are regarded as the one of the most versatile and useful of vegetables. They appear as the traditional flavourful brown or red globes of varying strengths, non-bulbous upright spring onions, small rounded onions for pickling, and shallots, which are extensively cultivated for use in both fresh cooking and in pickling.

Onions grown for pickling come from the common varieties but are bred to mature at a smaller size and are generally called 'picklers'. Most shallots have coppery-brown skin, whilst others have pinkish or greyish-brown covering. The French grey shallot, treasured by French chefs, is called a griselle and has a strong, delicious flavour.

Easily grown and with long storage life, modern onion cultivars offer all-seasons varieties for prolonged harvesting, but check planting times as cold-weather cultivars run to seed if planted in summer. Unlike other edible crops, which deteriorate once mature, onions store well in the ground and can be harvested when convenient. They serve well as a filler (from sets or transplants), make an attractive edging, and mix happily with carrots, salad greens and tomatoes. Their spear-like leaves form a handsome contrast to vegetables with broad or feathery foliage.

All onion varieties like a medium to light, well-drained rich soil. Sow seed from autumn to spring in temperate zones and in spring in colder regions. Seed is very small — sow thinly into furrows. Onions are ripe for harvesting when the foliage falls over and begins to brown. Lightly fork to break the roots, then leave to dry until the skin is dry and papery. Store in a cool place tied in ropes or in open trays.

Onions

Preferred varieties

Red varieties

'Early Californian Red', 'Sweet Red' (mid-season), 'Red Brunswick' (late season) are traditional favourites. For a pleasing contrast, plant a block of the old-fashioned pure white variety below alongside the red varieties.

White varieties

'Albion', 'White Globe' or 'Walla Walla Sweet': *Popular traditional varieties.*
Early season: 'Lockyer Early White' (early season), 'Gladalan Brown', 'Hunter River Brown'.
Mid–late season: 'White Spanish', 'Ailsa Craig', 'Creamgold Long Keeper'.

Dwarf varieties

'Purplette', 'Torpedo' and 'Red Italian': *Gourmet mini onions harvested small, but will reach medium size if allowed to mature.*

Spring onions (*Allium fistulosum*)

'White Welsh' and 'White Lisbon': *Sow thickly into open soil and thin by removing the largest to eat.*

Shallots

'Paris Silverskin' and 'Pear Pickler': *The strongly flavoured grey French shallot is called a griselle.*

● PARSNIPS (*Pastinaca sativa*)

An ancient vegetable from the eastern Mediterranean, parsnips reached Europe in medieval times and were introduced to North America by early settlers in 1600. Parsnips were a dietary staple before potatoes were introduced. A cold-hardy winter vegetable distantly related to carrots, their foliage is attractively dissected but of a lighter green and their distinctly flavoured roots, a creamy-white. The main difference between varieties is the length and shape of the root.

Parsnip seeds need cold to revive them from dormancy, so place in the refrigerator or freezer before planting. Sow seed (slow to germinate) directly into furrows in soil or in pots outside in early spring. Cover furrows with compost and keep seeds damp but not wet. Watering regularly and some shade will prevent premature seeding. Parsnips mature in winter.

Preferred varieties

'Guernsey': *French heirloom.*
'Tender and True': *Big flavoursome roots.*
'Hollow Crown': *Large roots.*
'Cobham': *English variety, sweetly flavoured wedge-shaped roots, quick to mature.*

Peas

● PEAS (*Pisum sativum*)

An antique vegetable dating back to 7000BC, the pea creates beautiful patterns with its angular silver-green foliage, dainty tendrils and sweet-smelling flowers of lilac, purple or white, which precede the fruit pods.

Climbing and dwarf varieties look attractive trained and supported on rows or tepees of twiggy branches or over pergolas. A versatile vegetable, peas appear as the tiny gourmet 'petit pois' varieties, the sugar snap, snow or 'mangetout' peas (harvested young and eaten pods and all), and the substantial larger-podded 'Marrowfat' varieties.

Peas like a cool growing season and most require vertical support frames. Dwarf varieties grown up tepee-style supports make excellent container and small-space plants. Sow seed 5 cm (2 in) apart into 4 cm (3 in) deep furrows, or in pots from autumn to spring in temperate zones, and from mid-winter to late spring in colder climates. Peas require fertile, moisture-retentive but well-drained soils.

Protect pea seedlings from mice, gastropods, and birds: a ring of coarse sand around each plant deters gastropods, and to keep out mice and birds, cover each seedling with an up-ended plastic drink bottle with its bottom cut out. Pea crops enrich the soil with nitrogen, especially if the roots are left in the ground after the crop is harvested.

Preferred varieties
Mangeout varieties
'Carouby de Maussane': *Attractive purple flowers and pods which remain on plant for weeks without going stringy.*
'Petit Provencal': *French heirloom harvested early, treasured for small tender peas with edible tendrils.*
'Snow Queen', 'Goliath', ' Oregon Sugar Pod' and 'Sugar Bon': *Also popular mangetout varieties.*

Traditional pod varieties
'Marrowfat'.
'Alderman Tall Climbing': *Prolific yield.*
'Greenfeast': *Adaptable to diverse weather and soil conditions.*
'Telephone': *Tall climbing peas, large pods. Prolonged cropping.*

Dwarf varieties
'Earlycrop Massey' and 'Massey Gem': *Quick to mature.*
'Bounty': *Mildew-resistant, suited to hot, humid climates.*

● POTATOES (*Solanum tuberosum*)
The world's fourth most important food crop after wheat, maize and rice, hundreds of potato cultivars have been developed since its origin in 5000Bc.

Although it is difficult to think of the humble spud as a decorative vegetable, its strong dark green foliage starred with white or purple flowers can be very attractive in season. (In 1773, French scientist Antoine Parmentier wrote a thesis extolling the potato's virtues. He presented a bouquet to Louis XVI at court, and Marie Antoinette set a dashing new fashion by wearing potato flowers in her hair!) The potato crop may be grown behind a row of tall beet or brassicas to conceal the foliage once it starts to die back and look unattractive.

Early varieties such as the traditional 'Concorde' may be dug while the foliage is still reasonably fresh and green. Either way, digging potatoes is part of the magic and mystery of gardening.

Seed potatoes or tubers come as early, early main, and main season varieties. Ensure the tubers purchased are certified virus-free. Plant tubers 5 cm (2 in) deep and 25–30 cm (1 ft) apart, in rows 60 cm (23 in) apart. This affords frost protection and facilitates 'earthing up' the soil over the developing tubers to exclude daylight, which causes greening. Gross feeders, potatoes need moist, compost- and manure-enriched soil and a sunny position. After harvesting, it is beneficial to plant the area with a green manure such as mustard or phacelia.

In a 'no-soil' or small edible garden, potatoes may be grown in old tyres, cut-down bins, barrels or large containers filled with enriched soil.

Preferred varieties
A selection of the following selection will give almost year-round cropping.
Early: 'Cliff's Kidney', 'Arran Banner', 'Concorde'.
Early main, and main: 'Rua', 'Glen Ilam', 'Aran Chief', 'Peru Peru' (interesting

Storing vegetables
In temperate areas, most root crops, including carrots, swedes and turnips, and hardy vegetables such as leeks and Brussels sprouts, can be left in the ground until required. In colder climates where the soil is waterlogged, heavy or freezes, crops may rot or be difficult to harvest. They're better lifted in early winter for dry storage.

Dry-storing
Sand
Root crops such as carrots, beetroot, swedes and parsnips can be stored in trays of moist, but **not** wet, sand. Lay the roots horizontally in layers of damp sand so that they don't dry out. Cover with another layer of dampened sand.

Potatoes
After harvesting, place potatoes in paper sacks and seal to exclude all light to prevent greening.

Nets
Crops such as onions, garlic and chillies can be plaited together and hung. Marrows, pumpkins and cabbages can be hung in netting bags or old pantyhose or stored, not touching, on open shelves.

Containers
Peas and bean seeds can be harvested and stored as dry food. Ensure the pods are fully ripe before harvesting. Lay them out to dry in a warm place. When the pods are dry and brittle, extract the seeds and store in containers.

Freshly dug potatoes.

small heirloom with purplish patches), 'Ilam Hardy', 'Red King Edward', 'Tahi'.

Other popular varieties include:

'Sebago': *High-yielding, smooth-skinned, white flesh suited to multiple cuisine purposes.*

'Desiree': *Red skinned, flavoursome pale yellow waxy flesh.*

'King Edward': *Gourmet multi-purpose potato.*

'Chat': *Small white tubers, available almost year-round, serve as baby new potatoes.*

'Kipfler': *Gourmet finger-shaped potatoes, delicately flavoured pale yellow flesh.*

● RADISH (*Raphanus sativus*)

A favourite of the ancient Egyptians, radishes are now grown worldwide, with some Chinese varieties weighing in at around 22 kg (50 lb).

Home gardeners prefer the tender little red crunchy varieties to enhance summer salads and stir-fries. Easily grown, hardy to both temperate and cooler climates and quick to mature, radishes make excellent catch crops or filler-in edibles. Radishes prefer a moist, fertile soil and regular watering, but winter radishes (which can be red, white or black-skinned) require well-drained soil.

Preferred varieties

'Purple Plum': *Heirloom French variety.*

'French Breakfast': *Mild, sweet and tender.*

'Long Scarlet': *Dark red roots.*

'Cherrybelle': *Crisp round mild-tasting scarlet globes.*

'Easter Egg': *Novelty variety with white, red, pink and purple roots.*

'Black Spanish': *Popular winter variety, extremely hot, white flesh.*

(Asian radish, see page 54.)

Rhubarb

● RHUBARB (*Rheum rhabarbarum*)

The earliest record of rhubarb dates from China in 2700BC; it reached Europe and North America around 1700.

Rhubarb is treasured in the ornamental edible garden for its height, large bold foliage and colourful edible stalks. One of the garden's most attractive architectural plants, gardeners often use it as a bold feature in flower borders. A perennial, remaining in one place for years, rhubarb produces great frills of fat reddish-tinted leaves. Though dramatic, they contain high concentrations of oxalic acid and are toxic and, as such, are often used to make organic pesticides

Rhubarb requires enriched soil, dies back in the winter, and prefers a cool, shady area. Harvest stalks on a cut-and-come-again basis for continuous cropping.

Preferred varieties
'Sydney Crimson': *Long crimson stems.*
'Wandin Winter': *Crops year-round.*
'Victoria': *Healthy strong greenish stems which colour crimson in cooler weather.*

- SPINACH (*Spinacia oleracea*)

First grown by the Persians, spinach was cultivated in China by the seventh century and reached Europe around 1100.

Young spinach.

An attractive and prolific crop that can be grown almost year-round, spinach has visually pleasing and highly nutritious rich dark green leaves varying according to cultivar, from shiny smooth, crinkled or round, to pointed or arrow-shaped. Rich in vitamins A and C, iron and calcium, quick to mature and of compact growth, spinach makes both a good catch and container crop.

Spinach prefers cooler temperatures, and unless well watered, may bolt in hot, dry weather. It is a useful vegetable for growing in the shade of taller edibles. The plants require rich moisture-retaining soil. Sow seeds in small numbers in spring through autumn and harvest leaves young and tender for continuous cropping. Spinach comes in both summer and cold-hardy varieties.

Preferred varieties
'Summer Green': *Fast-growing Japanese variety tolerant of short daylight hours.*
'Santana': *Popular bunching variety, small tender leaves, crops year-round in warmer zones.*
'Symphony': *Traditional winter stalwart.*
'Hector': *Good raw or cooked.*

European heirloom varieties
'Winter Queen': *Late season, large sweet leaves.*
'Amsterdam': *Large flavoursome leaves.*
'Bloomsdale Long Standing': *Tasty wrinkled leaves, heat- and cold-tolerant, prolonged cropping.*
'Viking': *Hardy, vigorous, quick to mature, upright in growth, well suited to container cultivation.*

- SWEETCORN/MAIZE (*Zea mays*)

Records show that corn (maize) was first cultivated in Mexico around 7000BC. Improved varieties became a staple crop in North America after 800AD and the vegetable arrived in Europe in 1600.

A stand of well-grown sweetcorn (or sugar corn) is a delight to the eye, the palate, and to the ear as it whispers and rustles in the wind. Few vegetables are more delicious than sweet, crunchy cobs of young corn. Early ripening varieties

Sweetcorn

make cultivation possible in all but the coldest of areas. A row of tall-growing sweetcorn looks attractive in the middle of a bed, as a border or temporary screen, and lends vertical accents within the edible garden. The ripened ears should be harvested when the tassels at the end of the cobs turn black.

A summer crop, corn requires an enriched soil and a sheltered, wind-free position in full sun. For continuous yield, make staggered sowings from late spring to mid-summer. Corn is a heavy feeder — for abundant crops dress with a general fertiliser throughout growth. Corn will grow in hot, dry conditions, but regular watering will produce sweeter and heavier ears.

Preferred varieties
Dwarf varieties
'Indian Rainbow', 'Gracillima' and 'Early Gem'.

Standard varieties
'Florida Supersweet': *Large cobs.*
'Hawaiian': *Sweet flavour.*
'Golden Bantam': *Heirloom cultivar producing more than two cobs per plant.*
'Miracle': *Produces cobs under adverse weather conditions.*

Ornamental varieties
'Anasazi': *Intriguing decorative cultivar with red, white and blue kernels.*
'Bloody Butcher': *Dark red cobs.*
'Ornamental Indian Corn': *Multi-coloured cobs.*

● SWEDES (*Brassicas napus*)
Of European origin, swedes are one of the hardiest of root crops and a useful winter vegetable. Easy-to-grow new varieties are disease-resistant and tasty, and are usually boiled and mashed with butter, cream and spices.

Swedes require deep friable moist but well-drained soil. Those maturing in cold conditions have the best flavour.

Preferred varieties
'Best of All': *Globe-shaped, yellow-fleshed, purple top, excellent texture, mild flavour.*
'Champion Purple Top': *Widely grown in the southern hemisphere, well suited to all temperate climates.*

● TOMATOES (*Lycopersicum lycopersicum*)
Originating in the Andean regions of north and central South America, tomatoes reached central and North America 2000 years ago and were introduced to Europe around 1523.

Modern tomato hybrids come in a diverse range of sizes and shapes and include cultivars suited to specific culinary requirements. In addition to the traditional reds, colours vary from green through yellow, to golden-orange and even black. Size varies from the giant fruit of the tall-growing 'Beefsteak' varieties, through medium-size fruit borne by prolific and reliable varieties such as 'Moneymaker', plum-shaped Italian varieties, to the tiny, deliciously sweet dwarf cherry or cocktail tomatoes.

A summer vegetable, tomatoes require a warm, sheltered position in full sun and moist, free-draining, well-composted lime-free soil. Water regularly during hot, dry spells — sudden deluges causes skin to split and flesh to spoil. Start seeds off in pots indoors and plant out in early summer. In colder zones, tomatoes are a popular greenhouse crop.

Preferred varieties
Dwarf varieties
The dwarf cultivars listed below all bear prolific, sweetly flavoured cherry-sized fruit.

'Sun Cherry' or 'Sweet 100' cultivars.
'Canary' and 'Red Robin': *Japanese mini-bush varieties.*
'Tumbler' and 'Tumbling Tom': *Prostrate varieties — stunning grown in an urn or hanging basket.*
'Tommy Toe': *Disease-resistant.*
'Baxter's Early Bush': *Prolific.*
'Microtoms', 'Canary' and 'Red Robin'.

Medium-sized fruit
'Oxheart': *Oval Italian variety.*
'Principe Borghese'.
'Russian Red'.
'Black Russian': *Heirloom variety, chocolate-black fruit.*

Large fruit
All bear large well-flavoured fruit. Many other hardy and abundant cropping heirloom varieties are also available.
'Beefsteak': *Meaty flesh.*
'Moneymaker'.
'Mortgage Lifter': *Disease-resistant.*
'Brandywine Pink': *Amish heirloom variety.*

● TURNIPS (*Brassica rapa* var. *rapa*)
An ancient dietary staple and easy to grow, turnips are a hardy vegetable, cold-tolerant enough to be planted in late winter. They're useful in the edible garden when little else is cropping for providing blocks of bright green leaves above white globes with pinkish-purple necks. Sow turnip seed thinly into light, loose soil; thin by pulling the largest roots and eat like radishes.

Preferred varieties
'Purple Top Milan', 'Purple Top White Globe', 'Early Purple': *White globes, rose-purple flesh on top, attractive border plants.*
'Snowball': *Fast-maturing, delicately flavoured, white.*
'Golden Ball': *Small yellow-fleshed variety suited to hotter climates.*

Tomatoes

Drying fruit & vegetables

Drying is one of the oldest methods of preserving food. Originally the main method was sun-drying, but nowadays, due to lack of space and uncertain weather, the most popular and efficient way of drying food is with electric dehydrators or in the home oven. Compact in size with multiple shelves and reasonably priced, electric dehydrators dry both fruit and vegetables. An added advantage is that home-dried produce is pure and natural, unlike commercially prepared food, which is treated with sulphur as a preservative and may also have added colourants. Drying food in the home oven is equally successful but takes much longer — inconvenient when the oven is needed for daily meals.

CHAPTER FIVE

Fruit in the edible garden

Perhaps one of the most ornamental and attractive sights in any edible garden is a tree laden with colourful ripening fruit. Certainly, one of the most sensuous garden pleasures is to reach out, pick and eat a sun-warmed fruit, letting the sweet juice trickle down your chin!

Great little trees

The average edible garden is usually small to medium size, so the following cultivars are all chosen for compact growth, or suitability for training as cordons or espaliers — to accommodate larger fruit trees since their growth can be kept to desired size.

Even if you don't have a garden, you can still grow your own fruit on a deck or patio area. Dwarf fruit trees rarely exceed 2–4 m (7–14 ft) in height but bear full-sized fruit and make handsome and productive container specimens which can be moved about to provide pleasing focal points or accent plants. In colder climates, pots can be moved to warmer positions in winter. Most nurseries offer fruit trees in both dwarf and cordon forms.

Multiple croppers

Ever mindful of saving space, hybridists have bred dwarf fruit trees of many types — some bearing the same fruit but others (called doubles or triples) bearing two or thee different varieties. Dual or triple combinations on one tree aid cross-pollination between trees and give extended harvesting. Many modern hybrids crop as early as their second season. Try to include early, mid- and late-season varieties of each fruit to give prolonged harvesting.

Pollination

Most modern fruit trees are self-fertile, that is, they don't require other trees for cross-pollination to take place — but some varieties do. Other hybrids are partially self-fertile: they will crop planted alone, but fruiting will be much heavier if cross-pollination from another tree takes place. If uncertain about pollination requirements, ask nursery staff at your local nursery or garden centre for advice.

Cultivation

Fruit trees do best in a warm sunny sheltered position in fertile moist but free-draining soil. (See also Chapter 9, pages 135–138 for pest and disease control.)

Espaliered fruit trees trained along wire frames utilise vertical garden space, create garden rooms, dividers and green 'walls' and provide prolific crops in mininal space.

Apples

Pears

Fantastic fruit

The range of fruit trees available is enormous. Space here allows the listing of only a few of the very best varieties of each fruit.

Key to fruit ripening times:
E — early season
M — mid season
L — late season
SF — self-fertile
S — medium to standard size

Pip fruit

● APPLES (*Malus domestica*)

Most dwarf apple trees have upright columnar growth. Fully grown they rarely exceed 2.5 m (8 ft) in height by 30 cm (1 ft) in width. The Ballerina varieties are among the world's most compact and popular apple trees.

Ballerina varieties

'Waltz': *Medium-large red-gold skinned dessert apple. Crisp juicy flesh, cooks and dries well.* M
'Ballerina 'Bolero': *Shiny green-gold skinned apple.* M
'Ballerina 'Polka': *Medium-sized greenish-gold apple. Crisp, juicy, full-flavoured.* M

Apple double cultivars

'Golden Delicious'/'Red Delicious'.
'Oratia Beauty'/'Granny Smith'.

Apple triple cultivars

'Golden Delicious'/'Braeburn'/'Royal Gala'.

● PEARS (*Pyrus communis*)

An ancient fruit, pears are native to Europe and Asia. The first cultivated varieties grew wild in prehistory and pre-Christian Romans began the hybridisation of improved cultivars. The European pear is now one of the most popular fruits in the world. Pears make shapely trees with glossy foliage, showy spring blossom and ornamental fruit.

Standard varieties

'Taylor's Gold': *International favourite. Golden-russet skin, flavoursome flesh.* L
'Beurre Bosc': *World-famous French variety. Brown-skinned, sweet juicy fruit.* M–L
'Concorde': *Smooth, sweet juicy flesh.* L/SF

Pear double cultivars

'Taylor's Gold'/'Winter Nelis'.
'Taylor's Gold'/'Beurre Bosc'.
'Taylor's Gold'/'Packham's Triumph'.

Stone fruit

● APRICOTS (*Prunus armeniaca*)

Small to medium-sized decorative trees with showy foliage and blossom and luscious fruit, the first apricots came from ancient China and Siberia. Dwarf cultivars are now available for container cultivation.

Dwarf varieties

'Aprigold': *Thrives in warmer regions. M*
'Golden Glow': *Hardy, heavy crops of golden fruit. Some cold tolerance. E/SF*
'Katie Cot': *Sweet, juicy fruit. E*
'Flavourcot': *Recent hybrid. Abundant cropper, large, juicy fruit, sweet orange flesh. E/SF*

Standard varieties

'Moorpark': *Richly flavoured juicy fruit. Espaliers well. Prefers cooler climates. E/SF*
'Royal Rosa': *Golden-red fruit. Disease-hardy. E*
'Tevatt': *Large sweet golden fruit. Prolific. M–L/SF*

● CHERRIES (*Prunus avium*)

A family favourite, cherries come in two varieties: sweet cherries (*Prunus avium*) and sour cherries (*Prunus cerasus*). Cooking cherries are rich in antioxidants. Most sour cherries are self-fertile and will pollinate sweet cherries.

Sour cherries (cooking varieties)

'North Star': *Large Morello-type fruit. Disease-resistant. L/SF*
'Morello': *World's favourite sour cherry. Disease-resistant. E–M/SF*

Sweet cherries

'Penny': *New cultivar. Prolific from early age. Large black fruit. Tolerates adverse weather. E*
'Stella': *Large sweet dark red fruit. Prolific. M/SF*

Sweet double cultivars

These are dual combinations on one compact tree with one variety grafted above the other to give an attractive tiered effect. Combinations bred to address all pollination issues. Prolonged fruiting.
'Stella'/'Lapins': *Two best-quality cherries. E/M*
'Burlat'/'Stella': *E*
'Stella'/'Rainier': *Best white cherry combined with red 'Stella'. M*

Apricots

Harvesting & storing pip & stone fruit

Almost all types of pip and stone fruit are ready for harvesting in mid to late summer. Gently twist fruit and if it comes away easily, it is ripe and ready for picking. As soon as fruit is harvested, transfer it to a cool, dark place and complete the chosen storage method as quickly as possible.

Apples and pears store well. Ensure that the fruits don't touch. If there is a possibility of frost entering the storage area, wrap fruits individually in newspaper or waxed paper. Specially moulded paper trays in ventilated cardboard boxes are also ideal for storage: many greengrocers will be happy to give you their empty boxes.

Pears which store well include 'Conference' and 'Doyenne du Comice'. Most apples store well but long-keepers include 'James Grieve', 'Granny Smith' and older heirloom varieties such as 'Cox's Orange Pippin'.

All pip and stone fruit can also be frozen, dried or preserved.

Olives

● OLIVES (*Olea europaea*)

Native to Mediterranean countries, olives have been cultivated since ancient times. Bearing abundant green to purple fruit, dense silver foliage and attractively gnarled branches, the olive is a highly ornamental tree ideal for the edible garden

Dwarf varieties
'Chemlali': *Shrubby tree. Prolific crops. Disease-hardy. M/SF*
'Koronekie': *Plentiful green fruit. M–L/SF*

Standard varieties
'Picholine': *Gourmet French olive. Abundant crops. Cold-
           hardy. E–M*
'Manzilla': *Famous Spanish cultivar. Prolific crops for both
           eating and cooking. E*
'A'Prugno': *Italian olive, attractive reddish-violet fruit. M*

● PEACHES & NECTARINES (*Prunus persica*)

Known to have been in cultivation around 300BC, peaches and nectarines are cherished summer fruits. They're closely related, but peaches have downy skin and nectarines smooth.

Nectarine varieties
Dwarf
'Nectar Babe': *Sweet juicy fruit. M*
'Flavourzee': *Yellow fruit. M*
'Garden Delight': *Red-skinned with yellow flesh, prefers hotter zones. SF*
'Trixie Nectazee': *Compact bush, yellow fruit. M*

Standard
'Lord Napier': *Internationally popular. Sweet juicy white flesh with dark
           crimson flush. E/SF*
'Independence': *Flavoursome fruit. M*

Peach varieties
Dwarf
'Bonanza': *Large fruit. SF*
'Garden Lady': *Large yellow fruit. Partially SF*
'Pixzee': *Large fruit. E/SF*
'Pixzee Peach': *Sweet yellow fruit. M–L*

Standard varieties
'Golden Queen': *World-favourite peach, sweet golden flesh. L*
'Tasty Zee': *Californian-bred cultivar, sweet fruit. L*
'Rochester': *Hardy to cooler climates. Large juicy yellow fruit. M/SF*

● PLUMS (*Prunus domestica* spp.)

The European plum originally came from western Asia and the Caucasus and reached North America by around 1629. Modern hybrids include the Japanese plum, *Prunus salicina*. A wide selection of both types for eating and cooking purposes is available.

Dwarf varieties
Dual combinations on one tree include:
'Coe's Golden Drop'/'Angela Burdett'.
'Black Doris'/'Santa Rosa'.
'Omega'/'Santa Rosa'.

Standard varieties
'Victoria': *Popular European plum, prolific, juicy yellow-red fruit. M–L/SF*
'Reine Claude de Bavay': *Gourmet French greengage plum, richly flavoured greenish-yellow fruit. L/SF*
'Duff's Early Jewel': *Large to medium dark red fruit, sweet golden flesh. E/SF*
'Santa Rosa': *Considered the Queen of plums. Large flavoursome purple-skinned Japanese plum, pinkish-yellow flesh. M*

Citrus *(Citrus* spp. *Rutaceae)*

Originating from ancient China and South-East Asia, citrus fruits include grapefruit, kumquat, lemon, lime, mandarin, orange and tangelo. Bearing glossy green evergreen foliage, richly scented flowers and abundant fruit, citrus trees are ornamental year-round and make handsome container specimens. In colder climates they can be moved to sheltered positions when required. Citrus require a warm sunny sheltered position in moist free-draining soil. A wide range of citrus varieties, grafted onto dwarf rootstock, is available worldwide.

Unlike other fruits, which have a fairly short and definite cropping season in both northern and southern hemispheres, citrus, in all temperate to warmer zones have extended cropping times, some fruiting almost year-round. The fruit also remains in good condition on the tree for extended periods. This, together with the fact that the expected cropping time in northern and southern hemispheres is completely in reverse, makes it difficult to give a hard and fast early, middle, late-season maturity time for many cultivars.

● GRAPEFRUIT (*Citrus x paradise*)
'Marsh Seedless': *World-famous cultivar, large finely-textured fruit.*
'Ruby', (also called 'Red Blush'): *Has pinkish-red skin and flesh.*
'Orlando: *Sweet seedless juicy flesh.*

Preserving fruit

In time-honoured tradition, soft fruit and berries may be bottled, puréed or made into jam, jelly and sauces. The pectin in the fruit gels with acid and added sugar to thicken the preserve. Some fruits are candied, crystallised or glazed using mixtures of sugar syrup, honey or treacle, and citrus peel, candied or crystallised, is a popular ingredient in cake making. Many fruits are added to pickles and chutneys and almost all fruits make excellent wines and liqueurs. Fruit soaked in spirits such as rum or brandy make deliciously alcoholic desserts.

Citrus orchard

Limes

● LEMONS (*Citrus limon*)
'Eureka', 'Meyer': *Prolific croppers.*
'Lisbon': *Hardy to colder zones.*
'Lotsa Lemons': *Drought-resistant.*
'Lemonade': *Lemon/grapefruit-flavoured flesh.*

● LIMES (*Citrus aurantifolia*)
Limes are small trees that are well suited to container cultivation. They come in two varieties: Tahitian (*C. latifolia*), which are cold-hardy, and Mexican (*C. aurantifolia*), which require temperate zones.

Preferred variety
'Bearrs' (syn. 'Tahitian'): *Compact almost thornless tree. Small, greenish-yellow, thin-skinned, seedless flesh.*

Kaffir lime
Grown for fragrant foliage which is treasured in gourmet and Asian cuisine.

● KUMQUATS (*Fortunella* spp.)
Introduced to the West in 1864, kumquats are compact shrubs with small, ornamental, orange fruit and glossy green foliage. The fruit is tart but makes fine marmalades and conserves. Delightful container specimen.

Preferred variety
Dwarf 'Calamondin' and 'Limequat': *Both highly popular, prolific croppers.*

● MANDARINS (*Citrus reticulata*)
Also called Satsumas and tangerines, mandarins are small, sweet, easily peeled oranges. Good croppers, they come in many varieties.

Preferred varieties
'Encore': *Firm, sweet aromatic flesh. L*
'Clementine': *World-popular variety. Superb small ornamental tree, deep orange flavourful fruit. Cold-hardy. Striking container specimen.*
'Nova': *Almost seedless, tender juicy full-flavoured fruit.*

Japanese Satsumas
Highly ornamental and productive small trees with weeping form.
'Miyagawa Wase': *Most popular Japanese Satsuma. Easily peeled, large flattish sweet fruit.*

● ORANGES (*Citrus* spp.)
Oranges fall into two groups: the sweet orange (*Citrus sinensis*), and the bitter orange *(Citrus aurantium).*

Sweet oranges

Dwarf varieties

'Bouquet des Fleurs': *Highly ornamental, intensely perfumed variety. Perfect in pots.*

'Chinotto': *Compact thornless cultivar. Ideal container specimen.*

Standard varieties

'Navel', 'Valencia', 'Jaffa': *World-famous varieties. Sweet juicy fruit. Prolific croppers.*

Blood oranges

'Maltese Blood', 'Tarocco'.

Bitter oranges

'Seville': *Tart flavour, marmalade orange.*

● TANGELOS (*Citrus x tangelo*)

Fruit originates from a mandarin/grapefruit cross. Famous for its sweet juicy rich flavour. Delicious for both dessert/juicing.

Preferred varieties

'Minneola', 'Orlanda' and 'San Jaciento' are all universally popular.

~~~~~~

Red currants

Soft, bush & cane fruits

Soft fruit bushes and vines are easily grown given a warm, sunny position, fertile soil and correct pruning. Fairly compact and with a few dwarf forms, once established, they crop abundantly for years. Cane fruit such as blackberries and raspberries with long arching canes need permanent support frames. Gooseberry, currant and blueberry bushes make attractive free-standing specimens about 1.25– 1.5 m (4–5 ft) tall.

● CURRANT FRUITS (*Ribes sativum*)

Black currants

'Magnus': *Large fruit.*

'Ben Sarek' and 'Loch Lomond': *Crop heavily.*

Red currants

'Gloria de Versailles', 'Ruby Castle', and 'Fay's Prolific': *Hardy abundant croppers.*

White currants

'White Versailles': *sweet delicate flavour.*

Blueberries

Freezing fruit & vegetables

Freezing is an excellent method of preserving food. Nutritional experts state that produce harvested young and tender, blanched and frozen immediately, retains far more nutritional value than plastic-wrapped supermarket produce which may have been on the shelves for weeks.

Freezing fruit

Soft fruits and berries are best packed in light layers of sugar, or in a sugar syrup, and frozen. To freeze individual fruits, lay each, not touching, on a tray and freeze. Once solid, pack them into desired containers. This method, suitable for both fruit and vegetables, is called 'dry-packing' or 'free-flow' and prevents 'clumping' and allows the fruits to be extracted individually or in small quantities.

● BLUEBERRIES (*Vaccinium* spp.)

Blueberries are rich in vitamin C and high in antioxidants.

'Southland': *Excellent flavour.*
'Bluecrop': *Hardy, drought-tolerant.*
'Herbert' and 'Stanley': *Popular old American varieties.*
'Bluejay', 'Sunshine Blue': New *UK-bred dwarf cultivar. Prolific. E*
'Dixi': *M*
'Delite': *L*

● BERRY FRUITS

Gooseberries (*Ribes uva-crispa*)

A long-lived shrub, the gooseberry gives prolific crops of fruit rich in vitamin A and potassium.

Preferred varieties
'Invicta': *Prolific, mildew-resistant.*
'Pax: *Dark red fruit.*
'Yorkshire Champion': *Sweet golden fruit.*

Blackberries (*Rubus* spp.)

Thornless varieties
'Merton Thornless', 'Oregon Thornless', 'Smoothstem', 'Loch Ness', 'Black Satin', 'Navaho': *Prolific crops, smooth canes.*

Loganberries

Loganberries, (*Rubus* x *loganobaccus*) are a cross of blackberry and raspberry. Red in colour and borne on long, trailing canes, loganberries have the flavour of both fruits.

Preferred variety
'Logan': *Hardy thornless plant. Best cooked. Cold-hardy.*

Boysenberries (*Rubus ursinus* var. *loganbaccus*)

A cross of loganberry, blackberry and raspberry. Growth habit is similar to loganberry with slightly sweeter purple-red fruit.

Preferred variety
'McNichol's Choice': *Spineless, prolific cropper.*

Cranberries (*Vaccinium macrocarpon*)

Closely related to blueberries, cranberries grow in moist, cool, wet regions.

Preferred varieties
'Crowley': *Ground-hugging American cultivar with large dark red berries.*
'Earliblack': *Universally popular. Red-black fruit, disease- and frost-resistant.*

Raspberries (*Rubus* spp.)

Modern varieties provide extended cropping periods.

Preferred varieties

'Delight', 'Glen Moy', 'Malling Promise': *E*
'Julia', 'Glen Ample', 'Malling Minerva': *M*
'Autumn Bliss', 'September', 'Malling Admiral': *L*

Strawberries (*Fragariax ananassa*)

A summer delight, strawberries come in diverse forms, from tiny alpine and wild varieties to large, red, juicy modern hybrids. Strawberries require full sun and need to be grown in mounds in moist well-drained soil. Mounding is important as the fruit rots if left lying on wet soil. Weed mat or straw around the plants will prevent rotting and gastropod attack. Propagated from runners, though it is wise to replant with fresh virus-free stock every few years. With early, middle and late-season varieties available, it's possible to harvest strawberries over extended periods in temperate climates.

Preferred varieties

'Cambridge', 'Red Gauntlet': *Large juicy fruit, cold-hardy.*
'Naratoga', 'Torrey', 'Tioga': *Thrive in warmer zones.*
'Sonata', 'Darlisette': *E*
'Cambridge', 'Darlselect': *M*
'Pegasus', 'Florence', 'Elsanta': *L*
Ever-bear varieties 'Flamenco' and 'Albion' fruit almost year-round
    in temperate zones.
Novelty hybrid 'Sweetheart': *Attractive drooping cultivar for
    hanging baskets and pots.*

Alpine strawberries:

Dwarf form makes alpines popular for border plants and hanging baskets.
    Miniature sweet fruit.
'Alexandria', 'Baron Solemacher', 'Reugen': *All crop well.*

● VINE FRUIT

Grapes

Grown by the Assyrians, Persians and Egyptians some 5000 years ago, and brought into Europe around 1500BC, the grape is one of the oldest cultivated fruits known. A traditional and decorative vine for the edible garden, there is a wealth of grape varieties with fruit of white, green, amber, rose or purple-black. New foliage emerges as large-lobed green fans which turn russet-purple in autumn. Varieties include those for wine-making and dessert or table grapes.

Grapevines have a vigorous spreading habit but can be espaliered in smaller gardens or trained up over vertical supports. The vine requires full sun and hot, dry summers to ripen the fruit and a fertile, well-drained soil. Tolerant of cold winters.

Raspberries

Strawberries

Grapes

Seedless dessert varieties
'Thompson': *Large clusters of sweet green-gold fruit. E–M*
'Ruby': *Big clusters of sweet reddish-black fruit. M–L*
'Himrod': *Honey-flavoured seedless green fruit. Cold-hardy.*

Other varieties
'Buffalo': *Considered the finest dessert grape but also makes fine ruby-red
    wine. Very sweet black berries.*
'Steuben': *Prolific cropper, sweet spicy reddish-black fruit. Hardy. Disease-
    resistant.*

Recommended for home gardens
'Isabella': *New Zealand/American cross. Large spicy blue-black berries with
    jelly-like texture.*

Wine grapes
'Sauvignon Blanc': *World-famous New Zealand variety. Easy to grow. Heat-
    tolerant.*
'Pinot Noir': *Small bunches of red-black berries. Thrives in areas with hot days,
    cool nights.*
'Pinot Gris': *White grape popular with both commercial and home gardeners.
    Prefers colder climates.*
'Reisling': *Creates an elegant wine, fresh-fruit full-bodied flavour. Hardy. Cold-
    tolerant.*

Kiwifruit
Also known as the Chinese gooseberry, kiwifruit can be grown in most
temperate climates. Requires a warm, sunny, sheltered position and well-
drained soil. Vine is vigorous and useful for covering walls and fences.

Preferred varieties
'Hayward', 'Abbott' and 'Bruno' are female varieties. 'Matura' and 'Tomuri' are
    male plants suitable for pollinating the latter.
'Jenny': *The only self-fertile kiwifruit. Recommended for home gardens where
    space allows only one vine.*

Passionfruit (*Passiflora* spp.)
Passionfruit are a family of perennial climbers with tendrils, lush green,
deeply lobed leaves and exotic flowers of white, greenish-white through
pink to lavender-purple. The rounded purple-black or green fruit have a hard
parchment-like skin enclosing a juicy, tropical-tasting, seedy pulp. Best species
for the home edible garden is *Passiflora edulis*. The vine requires a humus-rich
moist soil in a warm sunny sheltered position.

Preferred varieties
'Nelly Kelly': *World-famous cultivar, dark purple fruit, golden flesh.*
'Panama Red', 'Panama Gold': *Popular varieties which crop well early
    in the season.*

Nut fruits

One of the oldest sources of food used by humans. Regrettably, with the exception of the almond, most nut trees are too large for the small–medium edible garden and many are not self-fertile, thus requiring space for another tree to effect cross-pollination.

● ALMONDS (*Prunus amygdalus*)

A compact ornamental tree bearing froths of pale pink blossom in spring, the almond requires warm summers and cool winters. The dwarf varieties below crop well and will fit into the medium-sized garden.

Dwarf varieties

'All-in-one', 'Robijin': *Compact, self-fertile trees to 4 m (14 ft).*
'Garden Elf', 'Garden Prince': *Compact growth. SF*

Other fruit trees

● FIGS (*Ficus carica*)

One of the first documented cultivated fruits and a real food of the gods! Often classed as subtropical, most figs are cold-hardy and grow in all temperate climates. Though deciduous, the tree is attractive year-round with large, bold foliage and gnarled branches. Fruit vary in size and shape depending on variety — round, egg or pear-shaped. Skin and flesh colour also varies from yellowish-white, to red and purple to black. The flesh is a soft, seedy, sweet, juicy and delicate pulp. Generally vigorous in growth, compact varieties of figs to 3 m (8 ft) are available. Figs can be trained well to espalier form or pruned to shrub-like size to make aesthetically pleasing and productive container specimens.

Dwarf variety

'Crnica': *Small compact tree. Heavy cropper. Chocolate-brown fruit. M–L*

Standard varieties

'Brunswick': *Hardy. Tolerates colder climates. M/SF*
'Brown Turkey': *Crops twice yearly in warm zones. Large purple-brown sugary fruit. M/SF*
'Black Ischia': *Hardy and prolific. Rounded richly flavoured purple-black, fruit. Will grow in containers. E*

Ornamental trees

Other small ornamental trees and shrubs bearing edible fruit include crab apples (*Malus* spp.), the quince (*Cydonia oblonga*) and the japonica or flowering quince (*Chaenomeles* spp.). These elegant small trees or shrubs bear attractive blossom and foliage and give lovely autumn colour. They have an intriguing growth habit and polished bark, providing striking silhouettes in the winter garden. Quince trees produce highly ornamental bulbous fruit of red, gold or pale lemon, used for conserves and for indoor fruit and flower displays. The trees bear stunning blossoms on bare branches in late winter when seasonal colour is at a premium.

Figs

CHAPTER SIX

Herbs & flowers

Herbs

The ancients set great store in the medicinal and fragrant effects of herbs:

> *'Many herbes with their medicine and fragrant sweet smels doe comfort and as it were revive olwayes ye personne's spirits . . .'* Paradisus Terrestris, *John Parkinson, 1597*

The writing of ancient herbalists such as John Gerard and Nicholas Culpeper form the basis of much of the physical and homeopathic medicine in our modern world. The medieval herb garden was the world's first pharmacy, precious for its collections of medicinal plants, and literally thousands of herbs were ground, mixed and infused to cure the sick. Many herbs were also steeped in water and boiled until a concentrated essence remained — a process called decoction.

Powdered yarrow, thyme and woodruff were sniffed like snuff to cure headaches and clear the head. Infusions of basil reduced fevers and coughs were soothed with syrup of honey and hyssop; colds were treated with horehound, sore throats cured with infusions of sage and rosemary. Valerian brought sleep to insomniacs, feverfew relief to migraine sufferers and the seeds of fennel and fenugreek were beneficial to nursing mothers. The virtues of herbs were considered almost limitless, especially where they pertained to digestion. Gentian and peppermint in wine were taken for indigestion; rhubarb as a laxative; garlic in milk was a medicine to treat threadworm in children.

Herbal remedies passed from generation to generation undoubtedly worked, and many modern synthetic compounds in medicines contain the refined forms of the active drugs present in these plants.

Herbs have also been used since earliest times for insect pests, for culinary purposes, and for making pomanders and pot pourri.

Tiny tussie mussies (miniature bouquets) of fragrant flowering herbs were used by medieval judges — they buried their noses in them to dull the stench of the prisoners — somewhat hypocritical, since they themselves were not the most fastidious regarding personal hygiene! Nor were residents of draughty medieval dwellings and stone castles keen on bathing — they wore pomanders to disguise body odours.

The mistress of every castle and affluent home was skilled in the art of herbal medicine. Fresh herbs were strewn on the floors daily so that foot traffic bruised and released their pleasant odours to freshen often ill-lit, ill-ventilated, smoky rooms and to repel flies, lice and fleas.

Luxuriant edgings of lavender, chives and catmint create colourful borders through the potager herb garden, drawing the visitor towards the ornamental archway at its end.

Creating an informal tapestry, plantings of massed herbs release the fragrance of their essential oils to the sun. Red sage, *Salvia officinalis* var. *purpurea*, which has plum-coloured leaves with a soft purple bloom and dark blue flowers, dominates the front border. To the left, the massed pink flowers of common thyme are a pleasing underplanting for the purple sage.

In addition to use as culinary and medicinal purposes, aromatic herbs such as parsley, mint, thyme and sage were used as mouth and breath cleansers, and a bunch of these freshly picked herbs would be set out for the family's use each morning and evening. In times before refrigeration, herbs were added to food as preservatives, or to mask the unpleasant taste of spoiling ingredients. When meat dishes were less than fresh, they were strongly laced with herbs in a disinfecting capacity, in the hope of lessening the ill effects . . .

> *'It as been said that culinary herbs are for masking a flavour which shouldn't be there or for providing a flavour which should be there, but isn't'!*

A more positive interpretation is that herbs enhance the existing flavours of a dish and add further subtle nuances of their own. Today, when a chef requires a bouquet garni — a bunch of basic herbs — the selection might include chives, mint, chervil, rosemary, parsley, basil, marjoram, coriander, dill, sage, tarragon and thyme — perhaps topped off by colourful nasturtium flowers for garnishing.

Herbs have also long been used as companion plants in ornamental vegetable gardens. Their capacity to protect against pests and diseases, and to stimulate growth, is due to the intensity of the aromatic oils they contain.

Separate herb gardens

Traditionally, herbs were planted together in their own beds but were also used individually within the potager as companion plants.

If you wish to include multiple herbs in your planting scheme, a separate bed may allow a better display of the elegant formal compositions to which aromatic plants lend themselves. They create an eye-catching tapestry effect with contrasts of flower in season, foliage colour and texture.

When making a planting plan for a herb garden, calculate the height of each variety at maturity — they vary widely. Fennel or angelica, for example, are tall upright plants, the latter having bold and beautifully dissected foliage of glossy green. Clary sage (*Salvia sclarea*) is also a tall and unusual plant, bearing deeply veined and textured leaves and fragrant upright flower spires tinted white, pink and mauve. It's also a good idea to study which aromatics — such as mint and oregano — have invasive roots, and to be aware of those which self-sow readily. These herbs are better contained and controlled in their own separate garden or confined in containers.

Both of the designs opposite offer an aesthetically pleasing and productive display, and may be adapted in size to suit one's particular site and the plantings of herbs varied to suit personal culinary preferences.

Most herbs require warm sheltered positions in full sun, which is why herb gardens containing medicinal and culinary plants have traditionally been walled or bordered by dwarf hedges. Herbs give the best of their aromatic oils in the micro-climate created by an enclosed area in full sunshine. Step into such a herb garden and instantly become as drowsy and intoxicated as the bees! Herbs require light fertile well-drained soils and need to be harvested frequently to promote constant new growth.

The design for the central herb beds (at right) may be adapted from either square or rectangular shapes. The beds form a pair of both culinary and fragrant borders alongside a pathway. Each half may be used separately within other areas (such as the four corners or two diagonally opposite corners) of the potager. Care must be taken to place the taller herbs, such as borage, common fennel, geranium and pineapple sage, at the back of the beds near the hedges. This design is well suited to perennial herbs, which may be interplanted with annual aromatics according to the season.

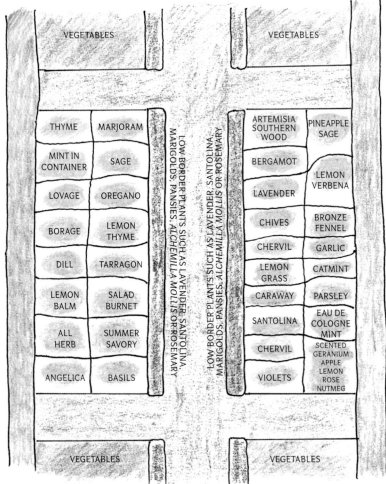

A herb garden is often used to create the centrepiece of the potager. The traditional circular bed shown at left is based on the simple wheel, or rays of the sun, designs which were popular in medieval times. The design works equally well laid out in bricks or as an open bed bordered by dwarf hedges of box, lonicera or lavenders. A variation which is visually pleasing is to encircle the central ring with hedging synonymous to the outer. This design is best planted with herbs of low to medium height. The plantings are suggestions only, and may be varied to suit individual climate and preference.

Basil, standardised rosemary bushes, parsley and dill (front) are ideal companions for tomatoes and other vegetables in this colourful garden.

Herbal harvest

Collect herbs for drying and storing in mid-summer while they are at their peak. Cut them on a dry day but not if they're wilting in the heat as the heat of the sun will have dissipated the essential oils which give herbs their distinctive flavour. Pick small bunches of the best leaves, avoiding older leaves. Leafy herbs should be picked before the plants flower when the oils are at their most concentrated. Small-leafed herbs such as thyme and rosemary should be picked on the stem. Harvest large-leafed herbs, like bay, as individual leaves. If required for drying, pick herb flowers as they open. Collect herb seed when the pods are ripe and brown. Place the pods in paper bags to catch seeds as they fall.

Favourite edible herbs

The following herbs are those used most commonly in everyday cuisine. (See Chapter 9 for herbs as insect repellents or attractant companion plants.)

● BASIL (*Ocimum basilicum*)

Basil is a prodigious family and it's very easy to acquire a tastebud-tantalising collection. They require warm, sunny positions and moist but well-drained soils. Frost-tender, they're generally sown as annuals. Said to keep mildew off cucurbits.

Basil is an indispensable and decorative herb coming in diverse foliage colours, sizes and flavours:

- The stunning purple-black modern hybrid 'Purple Ruffles' is universally popular. For striking plant association, combine its garnet glory with the lime-green foliage of feverfew (*Chrysanthemum parthenium* 'Aureum').
- 'Dark Opal' is another purple-black-leafed basil.
- Basil 'Green Ruffles' is similar in leaf form and flavour to 'Purple Ruffles'. Height 60 cm (2 in).
- Other types of basil include anise basil, with pretty anise-flavoured mulberry-tinted leaves that give subtle flavour to salads and sauces. An upright bushy plant, its lavender flowers make edible garnishes.
- Bush basil (*O. minimum*) is a dwarf basil with small fine leaves, suitable for container planting. Crops most of the year indoors and in warm areas.
- Basil 'Fino Verde' is a pungent bush basil used extensively in Italian cuisine.
- Cinnamon basil (*O. basilicum* spp.) from Mexico has a distinctive cinnamon taste and odour.
- Genovese basil is a broad-leafed sweet Italian basil, suitable for drying.

● BAY (*Laurus nobilis*)

Bay is a shrub which was revered by ancient Romans for diverse decorative and culinary purposes, and for crowning poets and scholars.

It makes an attractive container subject and may be trained to make impressive standard trees, but will grow to a small bushy tree if left unclipped. Rich green glossy leaves impart an aromatic flavour to casseroles, soups and stews. Hardy to most soils, the shrub tolerates dry conditions.

● BORAGE (*Borago officinalis*)

Borage has luxuriant tiered foliage of greyish-green with a cucumber-like flavour which, when picked young, is used in salads or can be cooked like spinach. Drop the herb's exquisite deep blue black-eyed flowers into ice-cube trays to decorate and cool summer drinks, or use as garnishes. Borage requires well-drained soil in full sun. It will grow to a height of 1 m (3 ft); keep trimmed for compact growth. Self-sows freely.

● CHAMOMILE (*Matricaria recutita* syn. *chamomilla*)
Upright plant that grows to 30–50 cm (12–20 in) high with dainty thread-like foliage and small daisy-like flowers which are used to make herbal tea. Creeping (Roman) chamomile (*Chamaemelum nobile*) is an evergreen perennial with small daisy-like flowers and filigree foliage. Used as a ground cover, spreads rapidly. Self-sows and is hardy. The non-flowering variety, *C. n.* 'Treneague', makes a fragrant lawn or surface beneath a garden seat.

● CHERVIL (*Anthriscus cerefolium*)
Brought to England and Europe by the Romans, chervil is a low-growing (30 cm, 1 ft), annual rich in vitamin C. The plant has very fine, delicate foliage and heads of small dainty white flowers. Self-sows once established, making an attractive filler between vegetables.

● CHERVIL ROOT (*Chaerophyllum bulbosum*)
This is a hardy plant treasured by French chefs for its delicately flavoured bulbous stems and roots. 'Brussels Winter' is a compact cool-weather variety. Chervil varieties require semi-shade and moist soil to prevent bolting. Height 1.5 m (5 ft).

● CHIVES (*Allium schoenoprasum*)
In his fifteenth-century *Compleat English Herballe* the ancient herbalist John Gerard defined chives thus: 'Chives hath both the smell and taste of onion and leeke, as it were participating in both.' An indispensable culinary herb, chives are an attractive plant with thin upright rounded spears and lavender pompom flower heads, adored by bees, which make a pleasing colour foil against green vegetables. Height 30 cm (1 ft). Chives are a generally hardy plant, tolerant of most soils.

Chives make a striking edging in edible garden borders and if regularly divided, plants clump up quickly. Popular cultivars include 'Chives Buster' and 'Chives Broad Leaf'.

Chinese chives (*A. tuberosum*)
These have attractive white starry flowers and slightly flattened spears. Rich in iron and sulphur, the herb is a mild antibiotic and is believed to help digestion of fatty foods.

Ornamental vegetable gardens often incorporate herbs in a separate bed or as a central focal point. An antique chimney pot planted with tarragon presents a delightful design feature. Herbs include santolina (rear right), chives, red sage, salad burnett, white catmint, pink-flowered thyme, golden lemon thyme, golden oregano, basil, coriander and rosemary.

● CORIANDER (*Coriandrum sativum*)
Also called cilantro or Chinese parsley, coriander is extensively used in Thai, Indian, Chinese, Mexican, African, French and American cuisine. This ancient herb is mentioned in the Old Testament. An attractive plant with clouds of small white flowers, its delicate finely dissected foliage is eaten cooked or raw. Coriander seeds are ground as a spice and used in many forms of cuisine. Requires a sunny situation and moderately good soil. Height 45 cm (18 in).

One can almost smell the sweet and spicy odours which the sunshine has released from the essential oils of the plants in this luxuriant herb garden. The tapestry includes purple-red sage, variegated golden sage, rosemary, angelica, scented geraniums, catmint and bronze fennel.

- **DILL (*Anethum graveolens*)**
A native of the Mediterranean and southern Russia, dill is an attractive annual herb bearing fine, filmy foliage and umbels of yellow flower heads with a strong aromatic scent. All parts are edible and rich in vitamins. Self-sows and grows to a height of 90 cm (33 in).

    Fernleaf dill is a dwarf variety suitable for containers and small-space gardens. Grows to 45 cm (18 in) and is slow to bolt. Needs a dry, sunny position sheltered from winds.

- **FENNEL (*Foeniculum vulgare*)**
With a rich aniseed flavour, fennel seeds are crushed and used in both sweet and savoury dishes. Attractive filmy bronze foliage is used with salads, fish and meat, and as garnishes. Fennel self-sows freely and can become invasive and hard to dig up, so remove and destroy unwanted seed heads! Perennnial which grows to 180 cm (6 ft).

- **FEVERFEW (*Chrysanthemum parthenium*)**
Feverfew is from 'febrifuge', a medieval term meaning a medicine to cure fevers. The common variety has light green foliage and small white daisy flowers with golden centres. *C. parthenium* 'Aureum' is popular for its attractive light lime-green foliage. Feverfew, strong and bitter in taste, has been used for many centuries to relieve migraine headaches. Hardy to poor soils. Self-sows. Height 50 cm (20 in).

- **GARLIC (*Allium sativum*)** (See also Chapter 4, page 71.)
Garlic has been cultivated since ancient times and is one of the most valuable herbs known. Medical scientists and pharmaceutical companies all over the world pour millions of dollars into research, believing garlic can reduce cholesterol levels, inhibit blood clots, ease asthma, prevent strokes and treat tumours. Grown as an annual by splitting the bulbs into individual cloves and planting each year, garlic requires full sun and fertile well-drained soil. Height 30 cm (1 ft).

- **HORSERADISH (*Armoracia rusticana*)**
A hardy perennial that grows to 40 cm (16 in), the plant creates a clump of exotic-looking leaves. Roots are harvested once a year but can be invasive. The flavour of the grated root is so strong that it was called 'monk's mustard' in ancient times. Grow from crown cuttings taken from the top 5 cm (2 in) of the mature root. Requires rich moist soil.

● HYSSOP (*Hyssopus officinalis*)
Hyssop is a small (30 cm, 1 ft) evergreen bush deserving of more
recognition than it currently gets. It has small, narrow leaves and
stunning bright blue, pink or white scented flowers, which attract bees
and other beneficial insects. Leaves are cooked with beans, or used
in stuffing, soups, sauces and egg dishes, and for herb teas. Requires
sunny position and fertile well-drained soil.

● LEMON BALM (*Melissa officinalis*)
Has prettily indented foliage and small white flowers. Height 60 cm
(2 ft). Requires light trimming to keep the plant compact. Can be
invasive. The foliage makes good tea. Young leaves are a pleasant and
unusual addition to salads. Attractive variegated and golden-leaved
varieties are available. Hardy. Best confined in a container to restrict
root growth.

● LOVAGE (*Levisticum officinale*)
Handsome hardy perennial with hollow stems that can be used like
celery. The leaves have a spicy, peppery taste and are used in soups,
stews and casseroles. Seeds give spicy flavour to cakes, biscuits and
bread. Easily grown from seed or from root pieces, lovage requires rich
moist soil. Cold-hardy. Grows to 2 m (7 ft.)

Clumps of catmint and a border
of double white feverfew daisies
enclose beds planted with red
and green lettuces, beetroot,
brassicas, globe artichokes
and other vegetables. A red
brick stairway and weathered
sleepers bordered by perfumed
mignonette, red poppies and
yellow pansies create an inviting
entrance to the garden.

● MARJORAM (*Origanum majorana*) AND OREGANO (*O. vulgare*)
These herbs are closely related. *O. majorana*, also known as sweet marjoram, is
a half-hardy perennial making a compact bush 40 cm (16 in) high, with greyish,
round, aromatic and flavoursome leaves. Used extensively in Italian cuisine and
to flavour fish, cheese, tomato and meat dishes. Leaves also dry well.
    Oregano has a sharper taste with small, attractive, heart-shaped leaves
growing opposite each other and delicate pink flowers. It grows to a height of 60
cm (2 ft) and makes a good groundcover in dry soils, but can be invasive. 'True
Greek' is a popular cultivar.

Pot marjoram 'Sweet Marjoram' (*O. onites*)
An easily grown perennial herb (60 cm (2 ft), it has a delicate flavour and small
pale pink or white flowers attractive to bees. Marjorams require a rich soil and
warm position in full sun.

Mint

● MINT (*Mentha viridis rotundifolia*)
Commonly called 'roast lamb' mint and the most popular variety for cooking
and in jellies and sauces. The Roman naturalist Pliny wrote: 'it do stir up men's
minds to the most greedy desire of meat'.
    Mints are best planted in pots to confine their invasive root systems. Two of
the most decorative are the cream-green variegated apple mint (delicious with

Italian parsley

Storing herbs

To conserve their flavour and
aroma, store herbs in airtight
containers in a dark cupboard.
Most herbs can be dried, frozen
or preserved in oils and vinegars.
The latter method is good for fine-
leafed herbs like basil, thyme and
oregano which don't dry well. Other
soft-leafed herbs such as parsley
and mint can be stored in ice cubes,
which preserves their flavour and
colour. Whole sprigs of other herbs
can be wrapped in foil and frozen.
Herbs may be stored individually
or mixed. The traditional bouquet
garni used to flavour soups, stews
and casseroles is a bunch of mixed
herbs — usually containing parsley,
bay, marjoram and thyme. Tickle
your family's taste buds by making
up combinations of your own.

Herbs to dry: bay, caraway,
coriander, dill, fennel, lemon balm,
lemon verbena, marjoram, mint,
rosemary, sage, tarragon, thyme

Herbs to freeze: basil, borage,
coriander, dill, lemon balm, mint,
parsley, rosemary.

pork) and the fragrant eau-de-cologne mint, with dark purplish-green foliage — a
handful of bruised leaves in the tired gardener's bath does wonders for aching
bones! Hardy. Height 50 cm (20 in).

● PARSLEY (*Petroselinum crispum*)

Parsley is a universally popular biennial herb rich in iron and vitamins. Easily
grown, but seed is notoriously long in germinating — old garden folklore says
it goes to the devil and back first! Soaking seeds for 48 hours before planting
helps. Many decorative varieties are available, including 'Italian Plain Leaf
Parsley' (*Petroselinum hortense*), which, unlike common curly-leaf parsley, has
flat leaves that dry well and have a delicate flavour. Parsley leaves are excellent
in all cooked dishes and in salads. Stalks may be crunched like celery. Other
varieties include:

- 'English Summer' is a popular traditional variety.
- Hamburg parsley (*Petroselinum crispum* var. *tuberosum*) often referred to
  as 'parsnip-rooted parsley', this variety has roots resembling small parsnips
  which can be eaten as a winter vegetable.
- 'Parsley Triple Curled' has dark green leaves on strong compact plants —
  especially attractive for garnishes. Cold-hardy, producing new growth in
  low temperatures.
- 'Gigantic Italian' (*Petroselinum crispum* var. *neapolitan*) has big shiny deep-
  green leaves with a sweeter, stronger flavour than standard varieties. Height
  80 cm (2 ft 8 in).

● PURPLE PERILLA (*Perilla frutescens* var. *crispa*)

Known as shiso in Japan and 'summer coleus' in the USA, this herb is an exciting
addition to the ornamental edible garden. A colourful foliage plant, used
originally in Victorian bedding-out schemes, it is now a popular culinary herb in
oriental countries, especially Japan.

Both leaves and seeds emit a pleasant spicy cinnamon odour from an organic
compound within the plant called perllia aldehye, an oil 2000 times sweeter
than sugar. Wrinkled dark burgundy foliage, heavily veined with crimson-pink,
is sharply indented along the edges like that of the common ornamental coleus.
Height 50 cm (20 in).

Green-leafed perilla is a green form of the herb which has a pleasant peppery
flavour. Easy to grow, but the seeds need light and chilling at 5°C in moist sand
to effect germination. Pinching-out the flower spikes keeps plants compact and
encourages colourful fresh new foliage.

● ROSEMARY (*Rosemarinus officinalis*)

Growing to 120 cm (3 ft 4 in), this hardy, shrubby perennial with sky-blue flowers
and narrow aromatic grey-green foliage is loved by bees. The prostrate variety
looks superb trailing from the top of walls or large raised containers. French

chefs decree that roast lamb without rosemary is a culinary sin! Thrives in impoverished soils but requires good drainage.

● SAGE (*Salvia officinalis*)

A hardy perennial growing to 60 cm (2 ft), sage is available in three ornamental culinary varieties, with striking purple-blue flowers loved by beneficial insects.

One variety has purplish-red leaves, another yellow-flecked, and a third has beautifully variegated foliage of cream, pink and green. The yellow-leafed sage (*Salvia officinalis* 'Icterina') is hardy in most situations. Sages occasionally die back unexpectedly, but cuttings from the parent plant root easily. Sages require well-drained soil and full sun.

● TARRAGON (*Artemisia dracunculus*)

Described as 'the king of herbs', tarragon is a culinary must in any edible garden. Russian tarragon is said to be inferior in flavour to the French variety (*A. d.* var. *sativa*). The herb has finely dissected long narrow leaves which have no odour until cut. The Russian variety has panicles of tiny yellow-green flowers and needs regular light trimming to keep it compact. The herb is used extensively in fish, chicken and meat dishes, and also stuffing, salads, vinegar and mayonnaise. Requires a sunny sheltered position and well-drained light soil. Height 60 cm (2 ft).

● THYME (*Thymus vulgaris*)

Perennial, growing to 8–30 cm (3 in–1 ft), although a dwarf variety, 'Bush Thyme', grows to less than 30 cm (1 ft). Bearing pink or white flowers and small silvery foliage, thyme requires clipping to keep a compact shape and promote new growth.

Creeping thyme (*Thymus serpyllum*), 1–5 cm (1–2 in), prefers acid, stony soil and carpets flat surfaces or falls attractively over low walls. They are popular for planting between pavers as their rich pungent oils are released by foot traffic. Bees are particularly fond of thyme flowers so resist the temptation to walk over them barefoot!

Thymus pulegiodes ('Aureus') has variegated green and gold foliage. Though hardy to poor soils, all thymes need full sun and good drainage.

Drying herbs

Seed pods and leafy herbs dry best in a dark, warm, well-ventilated place. Lay herbs on racks or hang in bunches to dry thoroughly. Within a week, they should be dry enough to rustle. Strip leaves from the stems and store them in airtight containers. Shake loose seeds from the pods and spread out to dry, or place leaves between two paper towels and microwave. Timing varies for individual herbs: check that they're dry enough; if not, cook for several more seconds.

Decorative vegetables

Many vegetables also bear beautiful flowers. These include those of climbing beans, peas, broad beans, potatoes and the golden-yellow chalice-shaped flowers of the cucurbit family.

Onions, leeks and chives provide attractive blooms although, in the interests of harvesting, they're not usually allowed to flower. If you have space, plant more of a vegetable crop than the family requires and allow some to run to seed. You'll be pleasantly surprised at the enormous variety and beauty of vegetable flowers. Chicory, for example, sports enchanting daisy flowers of the purest blue. (For other herbs and flowers for potager cultivation, please see Quick Reference Guides, Chapter 8, pages 118–125.)

French marigolds, (*Tagetes tenuifolia*) deter insect pests and discourage nemotodes in the soil.

Flowers in the potager

The idea of decorative edible gardening brings a vision of bright flowers combined with vegetables; such intermingling was common in the cloistered gardens of medieval castles and monasteries, and from this evolved the English cottage garden. In Victorian and Edwardian days, various flowers were used as seasonal indicators. Cucurbits were sown when mock orange (*Philadelphus*) bloomed, tomatoes when hawthorn blossomed, and corn when apple blossom fell.

As companion plants, herbs and flowers bring both practical benefits (protecting neighbouring plants from pests and diseases — see Chapter 9, pages 130–131) and beauty to the edible garden, but as they mustn't overpower or compete with the vegetables, it's wise to restrict those that are invasive or self-sowing.

Another reason for growing certain flowers with vegetables is because they're edible. Flowers for garnishing salads include borage, calendula, lavender, rosemary, nasturtiums, roses and daylilies.

Flowers are also grown to make garnishes, aromatic oils, teas, vinegars and waters for cooking or salad dressings.

It is also believed that flowers grown in the edible garden have the same effect as herbs: the perfumes of the essential oils of certain flowers, when released by the sun, stimulate the growth of nearby vegetables, for example, pot marigolds (*Calendula*) next to tomatoes. Some flowering plants enrich the soil by adding nitrogen or mineral properties. Clumps of lupins sown among thirsty salad stuffs provide light shade and fix nitrogen in the soil.

Edible flowers which are perennials need a position where their roots won't be disturbed. Low-growing plants can be used as underplanting for fruit trees or used as edgings for beds of perennial vegetables such as artichokes, rhubarb or asparagus.

Valuable flowering annuals

Four popular flowering plants for the edible garden include pot marigold (*Calendula officinalis*), *Tagetes tenuifolia* (these boldly coloured French, African and hybrid marigolds, though related to the edible pot marigold, may not be eaten), borage (*Borago officinalis*) and nasturtium (*Tropaeolum majus*). In addition to being aesthetically pleasing and edible, they repel pests and attract beneficial insects, stimulate the growth of other plants with their pungent perfumes and, in the case of calendula and tagetes, discourage nematodes in the soil.

Borage

See Chapter 6, page 98 for information about borage.

Calendula (pot marigold)

Height 30–60 cm (1–2 ft). This hardy plant has many-petalled edible flowers of cream, yellow or orange which can be used as a substitute for saffron in rice, for stuffings, herb butters and garnishes.

Marigolds (dwarf)

Height 28 cm (11 in). Hardy, but prefer well-drained soils. The dwarf forms of the marigolds, *Tagetes tenuifolia* (not edible), have more delicate, less brassy colours than the taller French, African and hybrid cultivars and their petals have lovely velvety textures. They're used extensively in the potager as both insect repellents and attractants and for their warm colours, which contrast beautifully with the darker green of vegetable leaves.

Tagetes tenuifolia 'Lemon Gem' and 'Tangerine Gem' with citrus-like odour and flavour are both edible and make pleasant additions to salads and desserts.

Nasturtiums

Height 30 cm (1 ft). Nasturtiums come as both dwarf or climbing varieties and have attractive rounded and veined foliage, and gay red, orange and yellow spurred trumpet flowers, freely produced over extended periods. The old hybrid 'Alaska' has striking foliage marbled cream and green. Nasturtiums are sun-worshippers and hardy to dryer soils. They'll bolt and form abundant foliage rather than flowers if over-watered, so plant them with vegetables that don't require moist soil.

The tender new leaves give salads a pleasant peppery flavour and the seed heads, picked young and small, can be pickled like capers. Nasturtium flowers make dramatic garnishes in salads and cold dishes and look stunning scrambling up climbing beans and as an underplanting to taller tomatoes.

Decorative aromatics with showy flowers

An important category of decorative aromatics are those which also have showy flowers. Although traditional herbs are treasured for the medicinal and nutritional value of their oily, aromatic foliage, they often have inconspicuous flowers.

A much-loved and versatile aromatic family is the catmint group (*Nepeta* spp.), from the tall, white-flowered *Nepeta cataria*, to the prostrate, purplish-blue *Nepeta x faassenii* and the cultivar, 'Six Hills Giant', which makes luxuriant clumps to 1 m (3 ft) high and wide.

Catmints will flower again if regularly trimmed. All are loved by beneficial insects — and, of course, cats!

The yellow flowers of tansy (*Tanacetum vulgare*) make an attractive colour combination with blue-flowered catmint. The plant looks like yellow achillea but is smaller (60 cm, 2 ft) — it dries well for floral decoration. Tansy leaves

This exciting colour-coded edible garden offers an electrifying combination of vegetables, herbs and flowers. Petunias, New Guinea impatiens, parsley, celosia and the tall salvia 'Bonfire' make an underplanting of vibrant reds and pinks for a colourful clump of purple-red rainbow beet occupying the centre bed. To the left, crimson canna lilies and the burgundy foliage and red flowers of a perennial dahlia provide strong contrast with dark green and grey speckled zucchini foliage. To the right, dwarf beans and tomatoes are bordered with salmon-pink achillea flowers, red saliva and dahlias.

Above: Parsley and capsicum underplant vibrant orange-red zinnias and tagetes marigolds at left. To the right, an edging of calendula borders a row of dark purple basil, capsicum and beet. A stand of sunflowers provides vertical accent.

Above, right: Treasured from earliest times for its beauty and perfume, luxuriant borders of royal purple old English lavender billow over the pathway through this edible garden.

make an efficient organic pesticide. Self-sows freely.

Bergamot (*Monarda didyma*), also called perennial horsemint or bee balm, grows to a height of 60–80 cm (24–33 in) and has striking shaggy flowers of vibrant deep reds, purple or blue. Prefers moister soils.

Roses for vertical interest

Apart from our general enslavement by the rose, repeated plantings of standard, dwarf or miniature roses in the ornamental edible garden give both symmetry and vertical interest in formal designs. While (probably) a bit over the top in the home potager, massed standard roses are used in dramatic manner at Château Villandry in France. Each of the four sections of this large potager has 36 standard roses, many of rich dark red, above multicoloured squares of vegetables.

The rugosa roses of ancient lineage look wonderful in the edible garden, having heavily textured dark green foliage and single to semi-double exquisitely perfumed petals of red, white or pink. Hardy and disease-resistant, they rarely require spraying and need little pruning. The rugosas also have highly ornamental hips which are rich in vitamin C. The hips come in intriguing shapes and give vibrant colour in winter. Rugosas make excellent hedges or screens. Height to 1.5 m (5 ft).

A traditional must in the edible garden is the ancient *Rosa gallica officinalis* — 'the apothecary's rose'. From earliest times the clear, crimson-pink, richly fragrant petals of this unique rose have been used for medicinal and culinary purposes and for toiletries. Compact in size, the bush makes a striking centrepiece or focal point. Height to 1 m (3 ft).

Other favourite rugosa varieties include 'Blanc Double de Coubert' (fragile tissue-like white petals bossed with gold stamens), 'Frau Dagmar Hastrup' (silver-pink), and 'Roseraie de l'Hay' (intoxicating perfume and luscious, deep crimson-red petals).

Given good-sized tubs the rugosas make striking container plants.

Tall flowers for the edible garden

Tall flowers are valued for their aesthetic appeal, their ability to provide screens, dividers and vertical accents, and some for their edible parts.

Love-lies-bleeding (*Amaranthus* spp.)

I've never fathomed why this attractive plant genus is saddled with such a gruesome common name. Cultivated for years purely as a flowering plant, many amaranthus species are now grown in underdeveloped countries as a much-valued food source — the leaves are used as spinach and the seeds as a high-protein grain crop. Amaranthus have long been grown in the flower garden for their visually appealing and brilliantly coloured flower tassels and spires. Now that their food potential is realised, they've become both an edible and ornamental asset to the potager. Amaranths are usually tall-growing annuals readily available from nurseries and seed catalogues worldwide. *Amaranthus retroflexus* (redroot) has attractive red stems and is usually grown as a vegetable, height 30 cm (1 ft). The ornamental *Amaranthus caudatus* (love-lies-bleeding) and prince's feather (*A. hypochondriacus* syn. *A. hybridus* var. *erythrostachys*) both give grain, as well as dark crimson to reddish-brown flowers and tender young leaves. Height 1–1.2 m (3–3½ ft). The cultivar *A. cruentus* is also valued for grain production.

Sunflowers

The French artist Claude Monet planted whole walls of sunflowers in his garden for the sheer joy of painting them. Famous French gardener Colette Lafon (1873–1954) described sunflowers as having 'hearts like black enamel', and grew them draped with sky-blue morning glories — a strikingly unusual plant association. If you wish to try this, it's wise to confine any *Convolvulus* spp., which can be invasive, in containers or purchase a cultivated, non-invasive hybrid.

Hollyhocks (*Althea rosea*)

The tall-growing (1.5 m, 5 ft), old-fashioned hollyhock has been a traditional favourite in English and European potagers for centuries. Carried freely on the top half of the spire, flower colours range from white through to pastel pinks and rich reds. The cultivar *Althea rosea* 'Nigra' has flowers so dark they're almost black. The tiered height of this plant, and the contrast of its dramatic dark blooms against large light-green foliage, make a striking sight in the edible garden.

Globe artichokes (*Cynara scolymus*) and cardoons (*C. cardunculus*)

Growing to a height of 2 m (7 ft), these plants provide dramatic architectural interest in the potager. They bear large and flamboyant silver-felted foliage and their edible, globular, thistle-like buds, if left to bloom, become silken-tufted purple flowers treasured for floral decoration when dried. (See also Chapter 4, page 53.)

Jerusalem artichokes (*Helianthus tuberosus*)

This is also a tall handsome plant grown for both its edible tubers and vibrant golden-yellow sunflower-type blooms. (See also Chapter 4, page 53.)

The leaves of grain amaranths are edible as are those of foliage amaranths. All have leaf and inflorescence colours ranging from green through gold to burgundy.

A bed of port-wine-coloured amaranths is an impressive sight in the edible garden, their long tassels or spires of millions of tiny flowers offering dramatic colour contrast, form and foliage amongst more prosaic vegetable varieties. Birds love their seeds — an excellent distraction from tender new veggie seedlings!

Amaranths require soil with high organic content and thrive in a slightly acid or lime-free position since they have a high nitrogen absorption rate. They're drought-tolerant but frost-tender.

CHAPTER SEVEN

The no-soil & tiny-space edible garden

As living space diminishes in our modern world, houses become smaller and many people live in high-rise buildings and small urban dwellings. If your edible garden is in an inner-city courtyard, an urban 'pocket handkerchief', or on a 'no-soil' veranda, rooftop or patio site — read on! In these locations, the versatility offered by container gardening allows the small-space gardener the joy of having home-grown vegetables, herbs, flowers and fruit.

Creating edible gardens in containers

Almost all vegetables can be grown in containers and grow-bags (see page 113). Even a crop of potatoes can be grown in a 10-litre (2-gallon) plastic bucket, cut-down dustbin or an old barrel. Aware of ever-diminishing garden space, plant breeders are concentrating on hybridising vegetable varieties with compact growth habits, but big on yield. These days, we have an exciting range of gourmet baby vegetables and dwarf varieties at our disposal.

Carrots, radishes, beetroot, dwarf beans, aubergines/eggplants, courgettes/zucchini, cucurbits, broccoli, cauliflowers, capsicums, chilli peppers, tomatoes and onions all now come in dwarf forms.

Capsicums, chillies and aubergines grow on compact bushes rarely exceeding 1 m (3 ft), thus making decorative and prolific container or small-space subjects. Tomatoes, in all sizes, are especially successful in tubs, pots or grow-bags. Among the root vegetables, traditional and reliable crops such as carrots, beetroot, radishes, parsnips and kohlrabi all now come in globe-rooted forms which can be sown in shallower troughs and pots.

Most cucurbits require a container about 30 cm (1 ft) in diameter and 30 cm (1 ft) deep. They will require a trellis or support to climb up. A grouping of 3–4 dwarf bean bushes, or 6 climbing varieties at the foot of a tepee in a large container 30 x 25 cm (12 x 9 in), or in a small bed, will crop prolifically if picked regularly. (See Chapter 2, pages 30–33.)

The cultivation of 'vertical veg' leaves precious ground space free for underplantings of other crops, or for the grouping of smaller pots containing herbs and companion plants beneath.

Larger varieties of the taller capsicums, tomatoes, cauliflowers, broccolis, marrows, pumpkins and other cucurbits need large pots, 35–60 cm (13–24 in) in diameter and 25–40 cm (9–16 in) deep. Old half barrels, built-in planter

This productive and innovative small potager, where the traditional and modern stand side by side, illustrates bold design concepts in a restricted space.

Well-fed and watered climbing beans grow happily in a terracotta pot, providing both vertical accent and a focal point.

Below: These cheerful containers are planted with (right to left) red chillies, tall lemon grass, red zinnias, variegated apple mint, red zinnias, tansy, chives, lettuce, parsley, purple sage, rosemary, nasturtiums, salsify and blue salvias — the ultimate in 'no soil' edible gardens.

boxes or fibreglass water tanks (remember to insert drainage holes) hold small groupings of larger vegetables such as cauliflowers and single plants of sprouting broccoli which, with regular picking, will crop over long periods.

The dwarf broccoli 'Raab' is popular for growing in small spaces.

Two universally popular dwarf cauliflower varieties are 'Alpha' and 'Idol', which will grow just 15 cm (6 in) apart in medium-sized containers or small beds. Harvest when heads are tennis-ball size.

A grouping of one each of an early, middle and late-season variety will give almost year-round crops, even in the container garden.

Pots or troughs about 15 cm (6 in) in diameter and 15–20 cm (6–8 in) deep are suitable for smaller vegetables and herbs. Most troughs are approximately 20 cm (8 in) wide and vary in length from 30 cm (1 ft) to 90 cm (3 ft). These can be used for more shallow-rooting vegetables such as self-blanching celery, salad stuffs, oriental brassicas, beetroot, kales, silverbeet and spinach. Chinese greens are compact in growth and quick to mature, making them ideal container subjects.

Beet and spinach plants are perfect for container and small-space cultivation since they're shallow-rooted and have a vertical growth habit. For big healthy plants for cropping on a pick-and-come-again basis, grow one to a pot, approximately 30 x 25 cm (12 x 10 in) or space 30 cm (1 ft) apart in nitrogenous rich soil. Water regularly in dry weather to prevent bolting.

Even with a no-soil or tiny edible garden, continuous crops are possible if you budget space for a sunny, sheltered 'nursery corner' where seedlings can be raised. With seedlings to replace harvested edibles, the growing season is extended and the crop yield as fruitful as that from a larger garden.

Small-space gardening success

The following ideas will help produce good crops and sustained yield in limited space.

1. Position your edible garden where it will receive maximum sunshine.
2. Grow as many vegetables vertically as possible to maximise space.
3. Choose varieties that suit your own soil and region.
4. If your soil is heavy or poorly drained, build raised beds from timber or brick.
5. Make staggered sowing and planting for continuous supply of crops.
6. Grow vegetable varieties bred for small spaces or container cultivation.
7. Maintain and enrich soil fertility with dressings of manure and compost.
8. Keep pests and diseases at bay with a strict hygiene routine (see Chapter 9).
9. Grow beans and peas tepee-style for all-round exposure to light.
10. Ask nurseries to recommend prolific cropping dwarf varieties.

Above: Deep containers placed end to end create a bed planted with salad stuffs, beet and herbs.

Left: Courgettes/zucchini, tomatoes and zinnias grow happily in an old bath, a hanging basket supports a dwarf tomato, and other containers hold a variety of herbs and vegetables.

11. Use cloches and cold frames both early and late season to extend growing periods.
12. Sow catch crops between larger vegetables.
13. Golden rule — remember that containerised crops need plentiful sunshine and regular watering and feeding to maximise yield.

Making a mini-cloche and a row cloche

To protect replacement seedlings in pots early in the season, make a mini-cloche by bending a loop in a length of number 8 wire about the same diameter as the pot's top, making sure you've left a wire leg long enough to push into the growing medium. Draw a plastic bag over the loop of wire and tie to the pot with string or a rubber band.

To make a simple cloche for a row of vegetables already in the garden, bend lengths of number 8 wire into hoops to the desired height, that is, with enough head space to allow the plants to develop. Push the wires into the

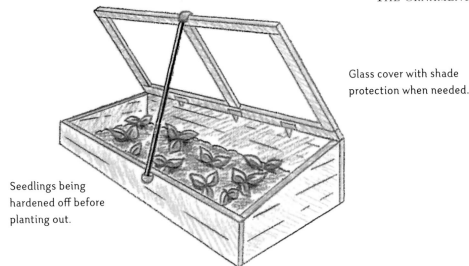

Glass cover with shade protection when needed.

Seedlings being hardened off before planting out.

One of the great advantages of container gardening is that plants can be moved easily, but a soil-filled container can be heavy. If you have a no-soil garden situation it is worth considering mounting all but the smallest containers on a simple trolley made of a flat piece of wood fitted with four furniture castors and a rope handle, which can help to avoid back injury. Tilt one side of the container, push the trolley under, then ease on the other side of the pot. Garden centres offer a range of custom-made devices on wheels for this purpose. The mobility of a container garden means that plants can be rotated, and groupings rearranged, so that the display is always at peak perfection. Tender plants can be moved to sheltered sites or indoors. (If this is impracticable, wrap the container in frost or shadecloth.)

soil at regular intervals and then thread an elongated sheet of clear polythene alternately over the top of one hoop, then under the next, until the whole row of hoops is covered. Tie or peg down the ends of the sheet at either end of the hoops so that the row of vegetables is covered by the extended cloche, and to prevent the wind lifting it off. Simple and inexpensive cloches such as this protect tender seedlings against slugs and snails as well as the vagaries of the weather.

Building a basic cold frame

The number of pieces of planking required obviously depends upon the desired size and height of your frame. The rear wall should be built higher than the front to accommodate taller seedlings. The side struts will need to be angled to meet the lower front wall. The cover may be constructed of a length of heavy-duty. clear polythene attached at either end to a light batten. A more basic design could be a square or rectangle of four planks of wood with an old window or piece of glass hinged onto or resting on top.

Suitable containers

Wood, plastic, terracotta, concrete, wire, basket-ware and other materials — the small-space gardener has a diverse range of containers to choose from. They must be able to withstand frequent watering, be strong enough not to disintegrate during moves and be complementary to both the plants they display and to the garden. Herbs and salad stuffs are often grown in window or built-in boxes of plastic or wood, though the latter become heavy when fully planted and wet. Most troughs for window boxes should have a planting depth of at least 50–60 cm (20–24 in) to accommodate root growth.

The availability of jumbo-sized pots, crates and barrels in a various materials allows the container gardener to grow fruit trees — even inner-city dwellers can luxuriate in spring blossom and home-grown fruit. Nurseries stock a wide variety of grafted and dwarf fruit trees. (See Chapter 5.)

Potting mixes

Success with all edible container plantings depends on the correct potting mix and moisturising agents. The health and growth of edible plants is in direct proportion to the medium in which they're planted. Cheap potting mix is a false economy — plants will be starved and spindly — invest in the best mix you can afford. Nurseries offer ready-mixed container mediums which include everything to promote plant health.

Nutrients and slow-release fertiliser granules are readily available and the free-draining mix allows the soil around the roots to warm up quickly, promoting consistent, healthy growth. Salad and leafy vegetables especially, need to grow quickly, as slow, stunted growth results in unpalatable, bitter-tasting crops.

Good-quality, ready-made mediums contain water storage granules, which have revolutionised container gardening by minimising the time and labour spent hand-watering. When added to water, the granules swell up to many times their normal size.

They retain moisture so that plant roots penetrating the jelly-like granules extract moisture as required. The crystals swell anew each time the container

Grow-bags

Grow-bags are flattish polythene sacks of potting mix and compost containing water-retention granules and slow-release fertiliser granules. They're designed to lie flat on the ground so that rows and blocks of plants or seedlings can be sown directly into them. To disguise the polythene, group smaller pots of companion plants such as marigolds, nasturtiums or herbs around the base. Grow-bags are excellent for the no-soil patio, verandah or roof-top garden since they can be disposed of or stored flat when crops are finished.

Clever use of space is illustrated in this small productive edible garden. Fruit trees are espaliered on wires along the timber fence and trellis panels support other vertical plantings. Raised beds formed with weathered sleepers are filled to capacity with healthy crops. Bed to the right features red and green lettuces, spring onions and a zucchini plant with bold foliage and golden flowers. A small stone duck provides a pleasant touch of whimsy. The handsome Burelli pot with a cold frame for raising seedlings to its left provides a bold central focal point. The rear bed is planted with broad beans, broccoli, onions and other crops.

The Eco Bokashi bucket

The Bokashi bucket is a modern, practical and convenient alternative method for converting kitchen waste into nutrient-rich liquid fertiliser and a semi-solid soil conditioner. The system is invaluable for small-space edible gardens, as the process is performed in a compact, bucket-sized container which creates ideal conditions for airtight (anaerobic) composting.

Bokashi is a Japanese term which means 'fermented organic matter'. Kitchen waste is placed in the bucket and a handful of EM Bokashi — a pleasant-smelling mix of sawdust and bran — is added. The bin is filled, layer upon layer with the EM and vegetative waste, which needs to be compressed with a masher to remove air pockets. A drainage lid in the inner base of the bucket allows the fermented liquid manure to seep into a storage chamber below, from where it is drawn off by tap.

When the bin is full, the organic matter will be fermented and resemble a soft liquid sludge. This may be dug into the soil around plants, used as a top dressing, and added to planter boxes and containers. Once mixed into the soil or potting mix, the final fermentation takes place.

Bokashi Buckets and the EM Bokashi mix are available, with full instructions, from major international garden suppliers.

is watered. Manufacturers also offer products for re-wetting dry mix and ensuring fast and even water penetration. Clay-based products for reducing moisture loss from terracotta and stone containers are also available. The substance is painted onto the inside lining of the pots, and a small hole left at the base to allow excess water to drain away.

If you can't make your own, it's more economical to buy potting mix and compost in bulk and bag it up in bin sacks. If storage is a problem, grow your edibles in grow-bags containing ready-mix. These may be stacked vertically until required and take up relatively little space.

If you can make your own potting mix, it should be sandy and porous but still able to hold moisture. Slow-release fertiliser and water-retention granules should be added. A good home-made mixture is two parts well-manured and conditioned garden soil, one part coarse sand and one part garden compost, and peat moss or a moisture-retaining agent such as vermiculite. Add 30 g (1 oz) of complete fertiliser (NKP 5:7:4) and 100 g (3 oz) of lime to each bucket of mix, and mix all components well.

Successive plantings & repotting

Try to have new seedlings always growing-on to replace crops which are being harvested. If storage space is short, use grow-bags which squash flat when not in use. It's possible to recycle old mix from finished crops but it should be treated before being used again. Add commercially prepared compost, slow-release fertiliser granules and water-retaining granules — but if you don't wish to mix your own, nurseries offer commercially prepared agents for revitalising used potting mix.

The flat-dweller's guide to composting

The following method allows the making of compost in a small area or in a well-ventilated corner of a shed or garage. (See Chapter 9 for compost-making on a larger scale.)

You'll require a wooden or plastic container (see page 133) with plenty of aeration holes. Fill the container in layers with roots, stalks and foliage of spent crops, vegetative kitchen waste, fruit and vegetable peelings (avoid cooked food scraps, which attract vermin and smell unpleasant), tea bags, coffee grounds, the contents of vacuum cleaner bags, shrubby and coarse prunings (to help with aeration), and discarded potting mixes from containers.

Add sprinklings of complete fertilisers or commercially prepared manure pellets between layers. Cover the mixture lightly, turn it once weekly and let it lie until the organic materials have rotted into compost.

If you can beg, borrow or steal a few bags of garden soil containing some worms, this will give you a head start. (See information on worm farms, Chapter 9, page 134.) Worms will work and aerate the organic materials and their castings are the world's best fertiliser. The worms will soon multiply, and as you use the matured compost, set portions containing some of the worms aside in a separate container for topping up a new brew.

Raise the container above the ground by standing it on blocks of wood or half-bricks and place a shallow tray beneath the drainage holes at the base to catch seepage which you can dilute with water to make a great liquid manure.

Liquid feeds & fertilisers

A good-quality potting mix will initially provide your vegetables with all the nutrients they need, but crops in containers require frequent watering, so nutrients quickly wash away. Replace with water-soluble fertilisers applied every fortnight or so. Most plants also benefit from a booster foliar feed, especially at flowering time.

Foliar fertilisers are readily available. Instructions per rate of dilution and application are given on the packaging. Commercially prepared foliar fertilisers often come with a feeder set, which contains a pack of plant food, a clip-on hose connector and a feeder jar. There is no mess or complicated mixing; the handy feeder jar is clipped straight onto the end of the garden hose and plants are fed and watered simultaneously. Foliar fertilisers should, however, be used only as booster feeds, the plants' main nutrition coming from well-fed, well-conditioned soil.

Take care with preparations high in nitrogenous minerals: they are fine for leafy vegetables, but will promote lush foliage at the expense of flowers in fruiting varieties. As discussed, some fertilisers come as slow-release fertiliser granules. Sprinkled into containers, they release nutrients over about nine months.

Nurseries also offer a comprehensive range of organic fertilisers such as seaweed-based, general-purpose liquid plant foods, blood and bone mix, and rose, tomato and citrus formula. Another good organic foliar feed is concentrated fish fertiliser, which isn't too high in nitrogen and the odour repels pests as well! These products are excellent aids to both container and open-soil cultivation. There's no excuse for fruit and vegetables grown in no-soil situations and small spaces not to come up smiling with rude good health and fruiting prolifically!

Containerised topiary & standardised plants

Containerised topiary specimens are invaluable for lending elegance and symmetry to the small-space edible garden and also enhance its basically formal structure. Smaller shrubs and ornamentals have been trained as

Nitrogenous fertilisers will promote the desired lush foliage on green leafy plants such as salad stuffs, spinach and Asian greens, but will do so at the expense of flowers and fruit on crop bearing plants.

topiary specimens and standards for many centuries. To the novice gardener, the art of pruning to shape topiary specimens may appear to be a somewhat technical and, on occasion, a dangerous horticultural skill to master, but elegant nursery-grown standards are exorbitantly expensive — always a compelling reason to try one's own hand. It's reassuring to remember in the learning stages that few plants will die as the result of incorrect pruning. At worst, your specimen may produce few flowers or fruit for a season or two, but it will certainly survive.

Be aware, however, that not all shrubs and trees make successful subjects for topiary. Some can't tolerate severe cutting and will eventually lose their vigour; others bear foliage that is too open to allow pruning to shape. The species below are generally slow-growing and densely leaved, and respond to trimming by quickly producing new shoots.

English box (*Buxus sempervirens*) and yew (*Taxus* spp.) are the traditional shrubs for topiary, but they're slow-growing. 'Mock box', shrub honeysuckle (*Lonicera nitida*) shapes just as well as box and in half the time. Holly trees (*Ilex* spp.) with attractive glossy leaves are ideal for clipping into simple shapes. Many of the thuja conifers (*Thuja* spp.) train into stout hedges but will also prune well to simple geometric shapes.

The artistry of topiary

Topiary is an ancient art that has become popular with modern gardeners. The more complicated shapes do require skill since the plants must be trained over wire frames, and one must, as the saying goes, possess one's soul in patience while the plants grow. For the enthusiastic gardener a steady hand and a little patience is all that is required in learning how to develop plant sculptures. It can take years to develop an impressive geometric head on a tall stem so read on, and when in a hurry, cheat!

- Choose a suitable tree or shrub (preferably two, for symmetry) with a strong, straight central trunk and a full, well-developed head.
- Remove all the lower branches to the height you desire, then trim the head lightly to a chosen shape. If you are a beginner, it is wise to stick to simple geometric shapes such as balls, cubes, columns and triangles, and a couple of passable topiary standards may be shaped in a few hours instead of years!
- It is also wise to provide a strong stake for taller standards, because the density of their heads can make them top-heavy and susceptible to wind. Use soft ties so that the trunk doesn't suffer injury.
- Remove any new shoots which appear on the trunk, and pinch back new growth on the head regularly to encourage more shoots and provide the density of foliage required to train the plant into a desired shape.

This cranberry has been patiently shaped and wound into a compact round topiary, but nevertheless is still producing fruit to provide additional interest and colour.

Other traditional shrubs which make pleasing standard topiary specimens include roses, conifers, camellias and bay trees (*Laurus nobilis*), upright rosemary (*Rosmarinus officinalis*), lavender varieties (especially *Lavandula dentata*, which has strong, upright growth and is quick-growing), citrus, orange blossom (*Philadelphus coronaria*) and hydrangeas.

There are many more small trees and shrubs which will clip well into simple forms and, in addition to providing vertical accents and focal points, they're highly ornamental, take little space and lend grace and elegance to the ornamental vegetable garden. Above all, they're well suited to life in containers.

A stone container underplanted with herbs makes an attractive centrepiece for this small circular edible garden. Pathways of mellow bricks are enclosed by box edged strawberry beds — netted to deter avian visitors! Climbing beans, tall white cleome flowers and old roses provide vertical accents and focal points.

Edgings of English box clipped into neat geometric shapes form strong accent points along the pathway leading into this potager of classical design. An interesting variety of vegetables, some of which are planted in symmetrical rows, grow in beds which are bounded by lower hedges.

CHAPTER EIGHT

Quick reference guides to planting design

The following summary of ideas for planting design is by no means exhaustive. Each gardener will have ideas of their own, and the plants suggested will perform according to geographical locations and climatic conditions.

Edgers for outlining beds & parterres

Edgers and dividers may be employed in a semi-permanent capacity as annual crops and flowers, or in a permanent capacity as perennial shrubs, herbs, hedges, espaliered fruits and vines, dwarf trees or soft-fruit bushes.

● LOW EDGERS

Annuals
Dwarf red basils, beetroot, dwarf marigolds, nasturtiums, ornamental kales, coloured lettuce, oriental brassicas, dwarf annual bedding dahlias and zinnias, strawberries.

Perennials
Cottage pinks, catmint, chives, bush thymes and sages, violas, violets, dwarf feverfew, lady's mantle (*Alchemilla mollis*), dwarf lavenders.

● MEDIUM-HEIGHT EDGERS

Annuals
Taller varieties of basil, bush beans, beetroot, red cabbage, bedding dahlias and zinnias, pot marigolds, summer savory, phacelia, celery, rainbow beet or chard.

Perennials
Lemon balm (*Melissa officinalis*), lavenders, box, *Lonicera nitida*, sages, winter savory (*Satureja montana*), rosemary, santolina and artemisias.

● TALL EDGERS

Annuals
Broccoli, cauliflower, cosmos, lavatera, sunflowers, amaranths, sweetcorn, taller marigolds, frames and trellises of sweet peas, peas and beans.

Perennials
Dahlias, dwarf hebes, French lavender (*Lavandula dentata*), rosemary, rue, santolina, *Sedum spectabile*, and ancient *rugosa* roses with sensuously scented flowers and highly ornamental hips; soft-fruit bushes, espaliered fruit, standard roses, rosemary, lavender or bay, and topiary specimens.

● **VERTICAL ACCENTS**

For overall balance, the edible garden requires plant groupings of varying heights. A selection of herbs, vegetables and flowers to add vertical accent include those needing support, and others that don't.

Needing support

Runner beans, peas, cucurbits on trellises, tomatoes, espaliered or cordon fruit trees, climbing nasturtiums and sweet peas, grape and passionfruit vines, honeysuckle, climbing roses and sunflowers.

Without support

Amaranths, angelica, artichokes, asparagus, bay laurel, sweetcorn, delphiniums, brassicas, canna lilies, cardoons, clary sage (*Salvia sclarea*), larkspur, green and bronze fennel, hollyhocks, horseradish, lemon verbena, *Phlomis samia*, standard roses, fruit bushes and topiary specimens, rosemary, rhubarb, ornamental tobaccos (*Nicotiana* spp.), verbascums (mullein), borage.

● **PLANTS FOR ARCHITECTURAL ACCENTS**

Artichokes, broccoli, cauliflowers, canna lilies, cardoons, sweetcorn, cucurbits trained to climb, bronze fennel, angelica, ornamental kales, sweet and hot peppers, rhubarb, rue, artemisias, *Sedum spectabile*, sunflowers, beefsteak tomato cultivars, borage.

● **BUSHY OR CLUMP-FORMING HEDGING & EVERGREEN PLANTS**

Box (*Buxus sempervirens*), *Lonicera nitida*, curry plant (*Helichrysum*), silver germander (*Teucrium fruticans*), dwarf hebes, bay laurel, hyssop, lavenders, rosemary, rue, winter savory, bush thymes and sages, santolina.

● **FOLIAGE FAVOURITES**

Feathery

Asparagus, carrots, dill, cumin and fennel.

Curly

Curly endive, parsley and kale.

● **SELF-SOWERS**

Borage, chervil, cosmos, evening primrose, fennel, feverfew, hollyhocks, lettuces, marigolds, nasturtiums, Californian poppies (*Eschscholzia* spp.), mustards, nicotiana, oregano, phacelia, violas, catmint, lady's mantle (*Alchemilla mollis*).

● **FAST-FILLERS**

Quick to mature plants include oriental brassicas, dwarf beans, feverfew, chervil, cosmos, land cress, mustard, phacelia, salad stuffs and bedding plants such as annual marigolds, dahlias, zinnias and nasturtiums.

Underplanted with vibrant red and orange nasturtiums, a wickerwork tepee makes an attractive support frame for a scarlet-flowered runner bean.

White-flowered standard roses combined with silver-leafed vegetables and herbs illustrate how well colours may be mixed in an informal manner to give produce with pleasure. The coppery-apricot blooms of the old rose 'Buff Beauty' spill over and complement the attractive copper fountain on the wall at the end of the pathway.

● PALETTE OF VEGETABLE, FLOWER & HERB COLOURS

Red, purple or violet-blue
Amaranths, aubergines/eggplants, purple basils, red Brussels sprouts, broccoli, red cabbages, kales, kohlrabi, lettuces, red chicory, bronze mustard, red orache, purple-leaf sage, sweet peppers and chillies, tomatoes, beetroot, purple-podded climbing beans, bedding dahlias with purple-black foliage, zinnias, roses and nasturtiums, strawberries, raspberries, blackberries, blueberries, gooseberries, artichoke and cardoon flowers, rainbow beet, runner beans, borage, lavender, purple-flowered peas, catmint, phacelia and chicory flowers.

Pink tones
True pink is an unusual colour amongst edible plants — a matter for regret since it is an excellent foil to the rich greens of vegetable foliage. Those offering pink hues might include roses, ornamental kales, pink, cream and green-splashed tricolour sage, the flowers of common marjoram, oregano and thyme species, Chinese artichokes, some dwarf beans, the seed globes of leeks (pale pink), and flowers such as dahlias and zinnias.

Yellow & gold tones
Yellow-leafed varieties of lemon balm, oregano, celery, rainbow beet and sage; the flowers and fruit of butter beans, peppers, chillies, squash, pumpkins, courgettes/zucchini and other cucurbits, some tomatoes; the flowers of brassicas, sunflowers, zinnias, bedding dahlias, nasturtiums and marigolds.

Silver & white
Artemisias, artichokes, cardoons, curry plant, lavenders, santolina, cauliflowers, white aubergines, Chinese chives, white kohlrabi, turnips, leeks and radish. Broad beans provide silver-green foliage and black and white flowers; many bean and pea cultivars have silvery foliage and offer white flowers, as do potatoes and white lavender. Onions, garlic, and chives also provide silver-green foliage.

It's fun to experiment with all sorts of floral, fruit and vegetable permutations, but learn which flowers are self-sowing or invasive to avoid unfair competition with the edibles.

~~~~~~

The quick reference guides that follow give the gardener immediate information on the life cycle, hardiness and colour of edible plants including vegetables, fruit, nuts, flowers and herbs. Information is given on whether support is required and on correct siting. Space doesn't allow for individual cultivation details — almost all edible plants require a humus-enriched, moist but well-drained soil in a warm sunny position.

TABLE 1: Vegetable growth guide

Plant	Lifetime	Hardiness	Site	Height	Spread	Support
AMARANTHUS	A	T	FS	T	M	M
ASPARAGUS	P	H	T	T	W	Y
ASPARAGUS PEA	A	T	FS	L	N	N
AUBERGINE/EGGPLANT	A	VT	FS	M	M	Y
BEANS, BROAD	A	H	T	M	N	N
BEANS, DWARF	A	T	T	L	N	N
BEANS, CLIMBING	A*	T	T	C	N	C
BEANS, HYACINTH	A	VT	FS	C	N	C
BEANS, SOYA	A	VT	FS	L	N	N
BEETROOT	B	H	T	L	N	N
BROCCOLI	A	VH	T	M	M	M
BRUSSELS SPROUTS	A	VH	T	M	M	M
BURDOCK	P	VH	T	M	W	N
CABBAGE	A	VH	T	M	M	M
CAPSICUM	A	VH	FS	M	M	M
CARDOON	P	H	T	VT	W	M
CARROT	B	H	T	L	N	N
CAULIFLOWER	A	VH	T	M	M	M
CELERIAC	A	H	T	L	N	N
CELERY	A	VH	T	L	N	N
CHARD	B	H	T	M	M	N
CHICORY	P	T	T	L	N	N
CHINESE ARTICHOKE	P	H	T	L	N	N
CHINESE BRASSICAS	A	VARY	T	VARY	VARY	N
CHOP-SUEY GREENS	A	H	T	T	N	N
CLAYTONIA	A	H	T	VL	N	N
CORN SALAD	A	H	T	VL	N	N
COURGETTE/ZUCCHINI	A	VT	T	M	W	N
CRESS, GARDEN	A	T	T	VL	VN	N
CRESS, LAND	B	H	T	VL	N	N
CRESS, WATER	P	H	T	VL	N	N
DANDELION	P	VH	T	VL	N	N
ENDIVE	P	T	T	VL	N	N
FENNEL	A	T	FS	M	M	N
GARLIC	A*	H	T	L	VN	N
GLOBE ARTICHOKE	P	H	FS	M	M	N
GOOD KING HENRY	P	VH	T	L	N	N
HAMBURG PARSLEY	B	H	T	L	N	N
HOPS	P	VH	T	C	W	C
ICEPLANT	A	VT	FS	L	M	N
JERUSALEM ARTICHOKE	P	VH	T	VT	M	M
KALE	A	VH	T	M	M	M
KOHLRABI	A	H	T	L	N	N
LEEK	A	VH	T	L	VN	N
LETTUCE	A	T	T	VL	N	N
MAIZE	A	VT	FS	T	M	M
MARROW	A	VT	T	M	VW	N
NEW ZEALAND SPINACH	A	T	T	L	N	N
OKRA	A	VT	FS	M	M	N
ONION	B	H	T	L	N	N
ORACHE	A	H	T	T	M	M
PARSNIP	B	VH	T	L	N	N
PEAS	A	T	T	VARY	N	C
POTATO	A*	H	T	L	W	N
PUMPKIN	A	VT	T	M	VW	N
PURSLANE	A	VT	T	L	VN	N
QUINOA	A	T	T	T	M	M
RADISH	A	H	T	VL	VN	N
ROCKET	A	H	T	L	N	N
SALSIFY	A	H	T	L	N	N
SCORZONERA	P	H	T	L	N	N
SEAKALE	P	H	T	M	M	N
SHALLOT	B	T	T	L	N	N
SKIRRET	P	H	T	T	M	M
SORREL	P	VH	T	L	N	N
SPINACH	A	T	T	L	N	N
SQUASH	A	VT	T	M	VW	N
SWEDE	A	H	T	L	N	N
SWEETCORN	A	VT	FS	T	M	M
SUNFLOWER	A	T	FS	VT	W	Y
TOMATO	A	VT	FS	M	M	Y
TURNIP	A	VH	T	L	N	N
WHEAT	A	H	T	M	N	N

KEY

Lifetime

A Annual, from seed to seed in one season

A* Treat as annual

B Biennial, from seed to seed in two seasons.

P Perennial, plant lives many years

Hardiness

H Hardy, will tolerate some frost

VH Very hardy, will stand severe frost.

T Tender, will tolerate slight frost if protected

VT Very tender, will not tolerate any frost

Site

FS Full sun

T Tolerant

Height

C Climber

M Medium, 50–100 cm (18–36 in)

L Low, 15–0 cm (6–18 in)

VL Very low, under 15 cm (6 in)

T Tall, 1–2 m (36–78 in)

VT Very tall, over 2 m (78 in)

Spread

M Medium, 50–100 cm (18–36 in)

N Narrow, 15–50 cm (6–8 in)

VN Very narrow, under 15 cm (6 in)

W Wide, 1–2 m (36–78 in)

VW Very wide, over 2 m (78 in)

Support

C Climber

M May be needed on windy site

N Not required

Y Yes

TABLE 2: Vegetable colour guide 1

Vegetables	Leaves GREEN Dark	Medium	Pale	Variegated	Silvery	RED Dark	Greeny-red	PURPLE Greeny-purple	YELLOW Yellowy-green	Stem Green	Red	Purple	Yellow	White
AMARANTHUS	Y					Y			Y	Y	Y			
ASPARAGUS		Y												
ASPARAGUS PEA	Y									Y				
AUBERGINE/EGGPLANT										Y				
BEANS, BROAD			Y							Y				
BEANS, CLIMBING		Y						Y	Y	Y		Y	Y	
BEANS, DWARF		Y						Y	Y	Y		Y		
BEANS, HYACINTH		Y						Y						
BEANS, SOYA			Y											
BEETROOT		Y				Y	Y			Y	Y		Y	
BROCCOLI		Y								Y				
BRUSSELS SPROUTS		Y				Y	Y			Y				
BURDOCK					Y									
CABBAGE		Y	Y			Y								
CAPSICUM		Y												
CARDOON					Y									
CARROT		Y												
CAULIFLOWER			Y											
CELERIAC	Y													
CELERY		Y							Y					
CHARD		Y				Y	Y					Y	Y	
CHICORY		Y				Y								Y
CHINESE ARTICHOKE		Y												
CHINESE BRASSICAS	VARY													
CHOP-SUEY GREENS		Y												
CLAYTONIA		Y												
CORN SALAD		Y												
COURGETTE/ZUCCHINI				Y					Y					
CRESS, GARDEN		Y												
CRESS, LAND		Y		Y										
CRESS, WATER		Y												
DANDELION		Y												
ENDIVE			Y											
FENNEL			Y											
GARLIC			Y											
GLOBE ARTICHOKE					Y									
GOOD KING HENRY	Y													
HAMBURG PARSLEY		Y												
HOPS		Y	Y						Y					
ICEPLANT					Y									
JERUSALEM ARTICHOKE		Y								Y				
KALE	Y	Y	Y	Y		Y	Y	Y		Y		Y		
KOHLRABI		Y						Y		Y		Y		
LEEK		Y						Y						
LETTUCE			Y	Y		Y	Y							
MAIZE		Y												
MARROW		Y		Y	Y									
NEW ZEALAND SPINACH		Y												
OKRA		Y				Y								
ONION		Y			Y									
ORACHE						Y				Y	Y	Y		
PARSNIP		Y												
PEAS		Y												
POTATO		Y												
PUMPKIN		Y												
PURSLANE		Y							Y					
QUINOA		Y												
RADISH		Y												
ROCKET		Y												
SALSIFY		Y												
SCORZONERA		Y												
SEAKALE		Y												
SHALLOT		Y	Y											
SKIRRET		Y												
SORREL		Y								Y				
SPINACH		Y												
SQUASH		Y												
SWEDE		Y												
SWEETCORN		Y		Y										
SUNFLOWER		Y								Y				
TOMATO		Y												
TURNIP		Y												
WHEAT					Y									

TABLE 3: Vegetable colour guide 2

Vegetables	Flowers						Fruit					
	Red	Pink	Yellow	Blue	Purple	White	Red	Pink	Yellow	Purple	White	Green
AMARANTHUS	Y		Y				Y					
ASPARAGUS							Y			Y		
ASPARAGUS PEA	Y				Y							Y
AUBERGINE/EGGPLANT			Y	Y						Y		
BEANS, BROAD	Y					Y						Y
BEANS, CLIMBING	Y				Y	Y		Y		Y		Y
BEANS, DWARF	Y	Y			Y	Y			Y	Y		Y
BEANS, HYACINTH						Y						Y
BEANS, SOYA					Y	Y				Y		Y
BEETROOT										Y		
BROCCOLI			Y							Y		Y
BRUSSELS SPROUTS			Y				Y			Y		Y
BURDOCK												
CABBAGE			Y									
CAPSICUM						Y	Y		Y	Y		Y
CARDOON					Y					Y		Y
CARROT						Y						
CAULIFLOWER			Y									
CHICORY				Y								
CHINESE ARTICHOKE		Y										
CHINESE BRASSICAS			Y		Y							
CHOP-SUEY GREENS			Y									
CLAYTONIA						Y						
CORN SALAD				Y								
COURGETTE/ZUCCHINI			Y						Y			Y
CRESS, WATER			Y									
DANDELION			Y									
ENDIVE				Y								
FENNEL			Y									
GARLIC					Y							
GLOBE ARTICHOKE					Y							
HOPS												Y
JERUSALEM ARTICHOKE			Y									
KALE			Y									
KOHLRABI			Y									
LEEK					Y	Y						
MAIZE							Y		Y	Y	Y	
MARROW			Y						Y	Y	Y	Y
NEW ZEALAND SPINACH												
OKRA			Y				Y					Y
PEAS				Y		Y				Y		Y
POTATO					Y	Y						
PUMPKIN			Y						Y			Y
QUINOA							Y	Y	Y	Y	Y	
RADISH						Y						Y
ROCKET						Y						
SALSIFY					Y							
SCORZONERA			Y									
SEAKALE						Y						
SKIRRET						Y						
SORREL	Y											
SPINACH												
SQUASH			Y						Y			Y
SWEDE												
SWEETCORN							Y		Y		Y	
SUNFLOWER			Y									
TOMATO			Y				Y		Y			
WHEAT			Y							Y		

TABLE 4: Useful flowers guide

Common name	Botanical name	Edible	Bee/butterfly attractor	Predator attractor	Pest repellent	Pest attractor	Green manure
ALFALFA/LUCERNE	Medicago sativa						Y
ANISE HYSSOP	Agastache foeniculum	Y	Y				
BABY BLUE-EYES	Nemophila insignis		Y	Y			
BASIL	Ocinum basilicum	Y					
BERGAMOT	Monarda didyma	Y	Y				
BLUE LUPIN	Lupinus angustifolius		Y				Y
BORAGE	Borago officinalis	Y	Y			Y	
BUCKWHEAT	Fagopyrum esculentum						Y
CALENDULA	Calendula officinalis	Y	Y	Y		Y	
CHERVIL	Anthriscum cerefolium	Y					
CHICORY	Cichorium intybus	Y	Y				
CHIVE	Allium schoenoprasum	Y			Y		
CHOP-SUEY GREENS	Chrysanthemum coronarium	Y	Y				
CHRYSANTHEMUM	Chrysanthemum x morifolium	Y					
CORIANDER	Coriandrum sativum	Y		Y			
COWSLIP	Primula veris	Y					
CRIMSON CLOVER	Trifolium incarnatum	Y	Y				
DAISY	Bellis perennis	Y	Y				
DAYLILY	Hemerocallis fulva	Y	Y				
DILL	Anethum graveolens	Y					
ELDER	Sambucus nigra	Y			Y	Y	
FENNEL	Foeniculum vulgare	Y					
FENUGREEK	Trigonella foenum graecum						Y
FIELD BEANS	Vicia fabia		Y			Y	Y
GARLIC CHIVE	Allium tuberosum	Y			Y		
GRAZING RYE	Secale cereale						Y
HOLLYHOCK	Alcea rosea	Y	Y				
HONEYSUCKLE	Lonicera japonica	Y	Y				
LAVENDER	Lavandula angustifolia	Y	Y		Y		
LEMON	Citrus limon	Y					

TABLE 5: Fruit and nut growth

Name	Height	Spread	Hardiness	Training						
				Fine	Bush	Standard	Espalier	Fan	Cordon	Tunnel
ALMOND	T	VW	H			Y				
APPLE	T/VT	VW	VH			Y	Y	Y	Y	Y
APRICOT	VT	VW	H			Y	Y	Y		
BLACKBERRY	VT	VW	VH	Y						Y
BLACKBERRY HYBRIDS	VT	VW	H	Y						Y
BLACKCURRANT	M	M	H		Y					
BLUEBERRY	M	M	VH	Y						
CHERRY	T/VT	VW	VH			Y	Y	Y		
CHESTNUT	VVT	VW	V							
CRAB APPLE	T/VT	VW	VH			Y				Y
ELDER	VT	VW	VH	Y						
FIG	VT	VW	H	Y				Y		
GOOSEBERRY	M	M	H		Y	Y				
GRAPE	VT	VW	H	Y						Y
HAZEL	VT	VW	VH	Y						
HUCKLEBERRY	M	N	ANN							
KIWI	VT	VW	T	Y						Y
LEMON	T	VW	T			Y				
MEDLAR	VT	VW	VH			Y	Y			
MELON	L	W	VT	Y						
MULBERRY	VVT	VW	VH			Y	Y			Y
NECTARINE	VT	VW	H			Y	Y	Y		
ORANGE	T	VW	T			Y				
PASSIONFRUIT	VT	VW	H	Y						Y
PEACH	VT	VW	H			Y	Y	Y		
PEAR	T/VT	VW	VH			Y	Y	Y	Y	Y
PHYSALIS	T	N	ANN							
PLUM	T/VT	VW	VH			Y	Y	Y		
QUINCE	VT	VW	VH			Y	Y			Y
RASPBERRY	T	M	VH	Y						
RED/WHITE CURRANT	M	M	H		Y	Y				
RHUBARB	M	W	VH							
STRAWBERRY	VL	N	H							
WALNUT	VVT	VW	VH							
WINEBERRY	T	M	VH	Y						Y

TABLE 4: Continued

Common name	Botanical name	Edible	Bee/butterfly attractor	Predator attractor	Pest repellent	Pest attractor	Green manure
LEMON BALM	Melissa officinalis	Y					
LILAC	Syringa vulgaris	Y	Y				
LOVAGE	Levisticum officinale	Y					
MARIGOLD FRENCH	Tagetes patula		Y		Y		
MARIGOLD MEXICAN	Tagetes minuta		Y		Y		
MARJORAM	Origanum majorana	Y	Y				
MEDDICK	Medicago lupulina						Y
MINT	Mentha spp.	Y					
MUSTARD	Sinapsis alba		Y	Y	Y		Y
NASTURTIUM	Tropaeolum majus	Y	Y			Y	
ORANGE	Citrus sinensis	Y					
OREGANO	Oreganum spp.	Y	Y				
PHACELIA	Phacelia tanacetifolia		Y	Y			Y
PINK	Dianthus spp.	Y	Y				
POACHED-EGG PLANT	Limnanthes douglasii		Y	Y			
PRIMROSE	Primula vulgaris	Y					
RED CLOVER	Trifolium pratense	Y	Y				Y
ROCKET	Eruca vesicaria	Y					
ROSE	Rosa spp.	Y	Y			Y	
ROSEMARY	Rosmarinus officinalis	Y	Y		Y		
SAGE	Salvia officinalis	Y	Y				
SAVORY, SUMMER	Satureja hortensis	Y					
SAVORY, WINTER	Satureja montana	Y					
SCENTED GERANIUM	Pelargonium spp.	Y					
SQUASH	Curcubita spp.	Y	Y				
TANSY	Tanecetum vulgare		Y	Y	Y		
TARES	Vicia sativa						Y
THYME	Thymus spp.	Y	Y				
TULIP	Tulipa spp.	Y	Y				
VIOLA	Viola odorata, V. x wittrockiana	Y	Y				

TABLE 6: Oriental vegetable reference chart

English catalogue	Botanical name	Chinese or Japanese name	Other names
AMARANTH, vegetable	Amaranthus gangenticus	Hinn Choy Shien-(hiyu)	Chinese spinach, callaboo, bayam
BROCCOLI, Chinese	Brassica alboglabra	Gai-Lohn, Kai laan, Fat Shan	Chinese kale
CABBAGE, Chinese	Brassica oleracea	Yeh choy	
CABBAGE, Swatow mustard	Brassica juncea	Daai gaai choy, Gai choy	Indian mustard, mustard green
CABBAGE, Santoh frilled	Brassica pekinensis	Yokyo Bekana	open celery cabbage
CABBAGE, Tah Tsai	Brassica chinensis	Taai goo choy	non-heading Chinese cabbage, Chinese flat cabbage
CELTUCE	Latuca sativa asparagina	Woh sun	stem lettuce
CELERY, Chinese	Apium graveolens	Kunn choi, Kintsai	Heung Kunn
CHIVES, garlic	Allium tuberosum odoratum	Gow choy – Nira	Chinese chives, Chinese leek
CORIANDER/CILANTRO	Coriandrum sativum	Yuen sai - Enshui	Chinese parsley, Dhania
CRESS, WATER	Nasturtium officinale	Sai yeung choy	
CUCUMBER, oriental	Cucumis sativa	Kee chi, Tseng gwa	
EGGPLANT, Japanese	Solanum melogena	Ai gwa	aubergine
GOURD, bottle	Lagenaria siceraria	Woo lo gwa	
GOURD, vegetable	Cucurbito pepo		
KOMATSUNA	Brassica campestris		mustard spinach
MALABAR SPINACH	Basella rubra	Saan choy	Ceylon spinach, slippery vegetable
MELON, bitter	Momordica charantia	Foo gwa	balsam pear
MELON, Chinese winter	Benincasa hispada	Too-gwa, Dong-gwa	white or wax gourd, ash melon
MELON, fuzzy	Benincasa hispada	Tseet gwa, Mao gwa	little winter melon
MIBUNA	Brassica rapa	Reng sheng cai	mibuna greens
MITSUBA	Cryptotaenia japonica	San ye gin	Japanese parsley, trefoil, Japanese honeywort
MIZUNA	Brassica japonica	Shui sai	Chinese pot herb, Japanese mustard/lettuce
MUSTARD, Mike giant purple	Brassica rapa	Mike Ta kona	mustard greens
MUSTARD, giant red	Brassica rapa	Aka takena	mustard green
MUSTARD, green in snow	Brassica juncea	Xue li hang serifang	leaf mustard
MUSTARD, SPINACH	Brassica rapa perviridis	Komatsuna	
OKRA, Chinese	Luffa acutangula	Cee gwa	angled luffa
ONION, bunch, white Welsh	Allium fistulosum fistulosam	Chang fa nebuka	bunching onions, scallions, cibol
PAK CHOI	Brassica chinensis	Bok choi, Baak cho	Chinese white cabbage
PAK CHOI, flowering	Brassica parachinensis	Tsai chim, Choy sum	Chinese flowering cabbage
PAK CHOI, flowering purple	Brassica parachinensis	Hon tsai tai	Purple-flowering Chinese cabbage
PEA, snow	Pisum sativum	Ho lon dow	edible podded peas
PEPPERS, hot	Capsicum frutescens	La chiao Laat jui	chilli pepper
PEPPERS, sweet	Capsicum annum	Tseng jui	
PERILLA, green	Perilla frutescens	Jisoo-Ao shisho	beefsteak plant, summer coleus
PERILLA, red	Perilla frutescens	Jisoo-Ao shisho	beefsteak plant, summer coleus
RADISH, Chinese	Raphanus sativus	Loh baak	Mullangi (India)
RADISH, Japanese	Raphanus acanthiformis	Diakon	Chinese turnip
SHUNGIKU	Chrysanthemum coronarium	Shingiku	Chop suey green
SENPOSAI	Brassica spp.		Japanese spinach
SPINACH	Spinacea oleracia		
SQUASH, spaghetti	Cucurbita pepo		vegetable spaghetti
TURNIP	Brassica rapa var. glabra	Pai lo po	
WATER SPINACH	Ipoema aquatica	Ong-chow entsai	water convolvulus

Young sweetcorn, clambering purple beans and leafy kale plants have been kept pest and disease-free with the use of companion planting, organic sprays, careful observation and manual removal of undesirable seasonal bugs.

Below: The provision of good host plants will allow beneficial insects, such as butterflies, to breed and feed.

CHAPTER NINE

Organic management

The organic gardener's philosophy

As gardeners we understand that in view of the need to feed an overpopulated world it would be unrealistic to imagine we could do entirely without chemical sprays and fertilisers, but as small-space gardeners we have the opportunity to reduce their use as much as possible.

The organic gardener believes that toxic pesticides and herbicides are harmful to the environment, to plant and animal life, and that they poison nature's food chains. Almost all chemical pesticides have indiscriminate killing power, that is, they kill both bad and beneficial insects. They are also systemic — they have to be absorbed by the plant tissue in order to poison it. This not only kills the insects which feed on or come in contact with the plant, but can also leave behind chemical residues harmful to human health when ingested.

Most chemical pesticides and fungicides have a withholding period, which means that a certain number of days must lapse before the crop is safe for harvesting. A small amount of chemical residue, however, often remains.

Organic gardeners wants to share their edible garden with myriad birds, bees, butterflies and insects, and eat spray-free food. They cannot do this if everything is smothered in broad-spectrum, toxic pesticides. To adopt such a philosophy, designed to eliminate only the unwanted pests or plants, non-specific chemical treatments with indiscriminate killing power are avoided and only alternative methods of pest, disease and weed control are used, in an attempt to follow nature's own controls.

Organic pest and disease control is sometimes said to be less effective than chemical control. It is true that most benign plant-derivative sprays (see pages 135–136), with the exception of Neemseed oil (page 136) are non-systemic and, as such, are not absorbed by the system of the plant and do not afford continued protection.

A certain level of pest numbers will always remain because organic preparations kill or deter only when they come in close contact with the bodies of undesirable insects. Organic sprays must therefore be applied to all parts of the plant, including the underside of the leaves, used regularly if necessary, and renewed after rain. The use of sprays can be minimised by inspecting crops regularly. For example, brassicas suffer seasonal infestations of caterpillars so it pays to turn leaves often and rub out the pests — the green thumb method!

Principles of organic management

The key to organic management in my own edible garden has evolved through experience and a combination of the following practices:

1. The use of insecticides, fungicides and herbicides made from non-chemical organic materials, that is, plant derivatives such as garlic and pyrethrum concentrates and Neemseed oil.

2. Awareness of the fact that even organic pesticides, if applied at incorrect strength or at the wrong time of day, can kill beneficial insects as well as pests.

3. The growing of certified disease-resistant plant varieties to minimise the need for spraying and the discarding of disease-prone species.

4. The growing of plants well suited to one's individual soil and climatic conditions and avoidance of those for which artificial cultivation conditions must be created. Grown in situations alien to their requirements, plants fail to thrive, will be weak and susceptible to attack by pests and diseases.

5. Employment of companion planting in conjunction with non-toxic sprays to attract beneficial insects and repel pests.

6. The avoidance of monoculture, which attracts large numbers of specific insect pests and diseases in one area. Plants of different species, set in rows or clumps, will both attract and repel specific insects, ensuring a natural balance between the two. In medieval days (before chemical sprays), gardeners did not differentiate between plants at all. A plant was a plant whether you ate it, smelt it or simply enjoyed its beauty — and they were all grown together.

7. Provision of plant hosts on which beneficial insects may breed or feed — a biological bug-eat-bug method of control by encouraging natural predators which prey on pests.

8. Acceptance of a tolerable measure of disease and pests controlled by organic methods, rather than a pest and disease-free garden achieved by the use of toxic chemicals. Be judicious about spraying. If there is little sign of pest or disease infestation, don't spray. Remember that beneficial insects will starve if they have no pests to feed on.

9. Care of the soil — the gardener's first line of defence — the welfare of our plants is in direct proportion to the health of the soil in which we place them. Grown in conditioned, nutrient-rich soil, plants will be strong and healthy and have an inbuilt resistance to pests and diseases.

10. The practise of crop rotation (see below). Plant edibles with the similar nutritional and mineral needs together. These sections are rotated around the garden year by year on a three-or four-year cycle. Planting crops on a rotation system avoids a build-up of plant-specific diseases in the soil and prevents the same nutrients being continuously extracted until crops fail. The more often crops are rotated the healthier both soil and vegetables will be.

Set behind hedges of mock box, 'Baggeson's Gold', edible plants in this small potager are kept healthy with companion plantings of flowers which attract beneficial insects and with the use of non-toxic sprays — if required.

Crop rotation

Crop rotation is immensely important because some plants actually put minerals or nitrogen into the ground as they grow. Crop rotation needn't cramp your style. It may seem difficult to achieve the colour schemes and plant contrasts desired if all you can grow in one bed are cabbages, but as we've seen, a delightful variety of brassicas may be grown together — wine-red and silver-blue cabbages, pale green or dark green, smooth skinned or crinkly skinned, and all those attractive oriental varieties which don't look like cabbages at all!

Densely planted, this bed contains a wide range of thriving vegetables with diverse foliage colours and textures. By growing different edible plants in each bed over two or three years, crop rotation is practised. This prevents a build up of pests specific to similar plants and prevents the same nutrients being continuously extracted from the soil.

Crop rotation plan

Year 1
- Bed 1: Grow root crops (salsify, parsnips, carrots, beetroot). Don't add lime to or manure this area.
- Bed 2: Sow potatoes. Add plenty of manure but no lime.
- Bed 3: Grow other crops (celery, onions, peas, cucumber, pumpkins, sweetcorn, salad crops). Check soil acidity and add lime if necessary. Manure well.
- Bed 4: Plant brassicas (cabbages, broccoli, kales, Brussels sprouts, cauliflowers, radish, turnips, kohlrabi). Dress with lime but only add manure if soil is short of organic matter.

Year 2
- Bed 1: Sow potatoes.
- Bed 2: Grow other crops.
- Bed 3: Grow brassicas.
- Bed 4: Root crops.

Year 3
- Bed 1: Grow other crops.
- Bed 2: Plant brassicas.
- Bed 3: Root crops.
- Bed 4: Grow potatoes.

Year 4
- Bed 1: Grow brassicas.
- Bed 2: Grow root crops.
- Bed 3: Grow potatoes.
- Bed 4: Grow other crops.

Year 5
- As for year 1.

Where there are multiple beds, these divisions need not be followed rigidly as long as the crops are rotated over at least three years. The golden rule is — the longer the time before a crop is reintroduced to the same bed, the better.

Insects & biological control
Bug-eat-bug

Beneficial insects exert natural control in the garden by eating those that are pests. If they are eliminated by non-specific pesticides, or by organic preparations used at incorrect strength, any pests that survive will flourish. With their natural predators destroyed, they breed unchecked and one becomes locked in an unrelenting cycle of synthetic chemical control.

Similarly, if total annihilation of pestiferous insects takes place, beneficial insects that have survived will starve, leading in turn to poor pollination rate and low fertility throughout the garden.

Instead of asking yourself 'Why have I so many pests?' instead, ask yourself, 'Why have I so few predators?'

The aim is to maintain a happy balance by using the correct spray at correct strength, at the correct time, and only on those areas in which an unacceptable level of undesirable insect infestation or disease is seen.

The organic gardener has a different perspective of the old adage 'prevention is better than cure'; he or she does not spray the entire garden, but works instead towards a live-and-let-live philosophy — the balance of good and bad insects existing for mutual benefit, which is what nature intended before humankind destroyed that balance.

Plant hosts for beneficial insects

The bug-eat-bug approach encourages the provision of host plants for both types of insects. Organic gardeners back up their spray programme with companion planting by combining herbs and other plants that will attract or repel insects as required. Specific varieties are used as host plants on which beneficial insects can feed and breed. One of the most valuable of these is *Phacelia tanacetifolia*, which is used extensively in horticulture and agriculture for the control of white butterfly and aphid pests.

Phacelia is a beautiful plant which grows to 45 cm (18 in). It has filmy foliage and fluffy blue flower heads, freely borne over an extended period. It attracts that most voracious of predators, the hoverfly. The adult female hoverfly needs to eat pollen to bring her eggs to maturity — and must be assured of colonies of aphids on which to feed the larvae. The hoverfly resembles a honeybee in shape, but displays brilliant metallic colours.

Adult hoverflies have a short tongue, so in addition to phacelia — their favourite food — they'll breed and feed on marigolds, poached-egg flower (*Limnanthes douglasii*), and baby blue-eyes (*Nemophila insignis*). Hoverflies will also eat aphids, scale insects, small caterpillars and caterpillar eggs, so they are visitors deserving of bed and breakfast in any garden!

Phacelia also attracts other predatory insects, such as lacewings and ladybirds.

Phacelia tanacetifolia is one of the most highly valued and effective host plant for insects that prey on pests, and it is used extensively by organic gardeners.

Below: Poached-egg plant (*Limnanthes douglassi*) is a superb host plant for beneficial insects such as bees and hoverfly.

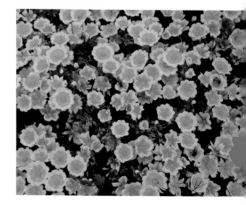

Attractive companion plantings of French marigolds, dwarf feverfew and calendula protect lettuce, tomatoes, onions, beet and other vegetables from insect pests.

Below: Nasturtiums (*Tropaeolum majus*) are both an attractant and repellent plant. They provide a host for undesirable insects, such as black aphids, thereby preventing them from infesting plants, but their strong odour also repels pest such as beetles and chewing insects.

The lacewing (*Micromus tasmaniae*) preys on aphids, mealy bugs, thrips, scale insects, moth eggs and mites, including those of the red spider.

Ladybirds are a precious garden resident. They're reputed to each eat at least 100 aphids a day and also relish scale insects, mealy bugs, leaf hoppers, whitefly, mites, the potato beetle and the bean beetle. Aphids are so predominant because there is a world shortage of ladybirds due to massive global usage of DDT in the '60s and '70s. Horticultural scientists say their numbers are increasing only slowly.

The food fetish of that other most beneficial insect, the praying mantis, includes caterpillars, aphids and leaf hoppers.

Companion planting — employing flowers & herbs for pest control

All strongly scented culinary herbs can be used to confuse pests, either by planting them close to the 'victim' plants, by cutting their leaves to mulch tender new transplants, or by steeping them in water to make organic insecticides. A handful of the leaves of feverfew (*Chrysanthemum parthenium*) spread around transplanted seedlings makes an excellent insect-repelling mulch.

One of the best-known flowers for pest control is the French marigold, which is not edible. It repels aphids, white-cabbage butterflies above the ground, and nematodes underground. The dwarf cultivars *Tagetes tenuifolia* are also said to ward off nematodes and to stimulate the growth of beans, cucumbers, aubergines/eggplants, melons, potatoes, pumpkins and tomatoes. They look wonderful under sweetcorn and tomatoes and make decorative temporary edgings or fast-fillers in awkward corners.

Other flower species extensively used as beneficial companion plants are pot marigold (*Calendula officinalis*), borage (*Borago officinalis*), and nasturtiums (*Tropaeolum majus*). In addition to being aesthetically pleasing, their pungent perfumes stimulate plant growth and deter nematodes in the soil. Calendulas are believed to deter beetles among asparagus and work against nematodes among carrots, tomatoes and beetroot.

Specific plants beneficial for pest control include:

- Artemisia: Though on the large side, artemisias have beautiful silver feathery foliage and pungent scents which repel flies and other insects pests from vegetables planted nearby. Wormwood (*Artemisia absinthium*), height 1.5 m (5 ft), makes an attractive shrub (cut it back twice yearly to keep it compact). Southernwood (*A. abrotanum*), height 1.5 m (5 ft) is a vigorous spreader. *A. schmidtiana* rarely exceeds 60 cm (2 ft) in height and width. The artemisia family is drought-tolerant and hardy in all but poorly drained soils.

- Borage (*Borago officinalis*): Repels pests but is also a powerful host plant for bees and other beneficial insects. It is said to improve the flavour of cucurbits and tomatoes, increase the disease resistance of strawberries, and to protect cabbage and kale plants from pests such as stink bugs and flea beetles. The plant also serves as an attractant for aphids, which might seem like an excellent idea for not growing it, but see how you feel when the borage next to your dwarf beans is liberally adorned with the pest while your beans remain totally unscathed! Since borage self-sows readily, remove and dispose of the pest-infested plants as soon as new seedlings appear.
- Chervil (*Anthriscus cerefolium*): Height 25–50 cm (9–20 in). Believed to protect lettuce against aphids, mildew, snails and slugs, and also to keep away ants.
- Chives (*Allium schoenoprasum*): Hardy herbs to 30 cm (1 ft). Believed to be particularly beneficial companion plants to roses, helping prevent black spot and mildew, and deterring aphids and other pests.
- Dill (*Antheum graveolens*): Annual to 90 cm (3 ft). Said to deter carrot fly, slugs and snails. Self-sows.
- Garlic (*Allium sativum*): Both garlic and the onion family have been valued since ancient times for their insect-repellent properties. For example, garlic makes an ideal edging for a bed of parsnips or carrots in the potager and as underplanting beneath roses in the flower garden. Garlic is now used extensively in the manufacture of organic insect-repellent sprays.
- Nasturtiums (*Tropaeolum majus*). Useful in both dwarf and climbing varieties. Set among brassicas, celery and cucumbers, nasturtiums deter beetles and aphids and are said to improve the flavour of cucumber, radishes and courgettes/zucchini. Some gardeners say that while nasturtiums repel woolly aphids, they attract the black variety, but others consider this good reason for planting the flower because it acts as a decoy plant. Lateral thinking — as with borage, better to have legions of the black pest on the nasturtiums than on the cabbages!

Other pest-repelling plants include tansy, mint, pennyroyal and wormwood. Basil is truly the gardener's friend (especially in the greenhouse) — bees love it; aphids, fruit fly, whitefly and the housefly loathe it.

Green manures

This practice involves growing plants and then digging them into the soil when they are mature either to improve its fertility and moisture retentiveness, or to be used as mulches when cut down. In addition to adding nutrients to the soil, green manures and mulches are also decorative in the edible garden. It's better to see a bed covered and protected by a green

Bee gardens

The provision of host plants for beneficial insects is essential to the health and fertility of the garden. Shrubs, such as buddlejas or 'butterfly' plants, attract bees and butterflies in large numbers, which vastly improves pollination rates and thus increases crop production. Common buddleja (*Agastache foeniculum*) with purple flower spikes and the buddleja 'Lochinch', which has graceful silver arched branches ,are both invaluable host plants for beneficial insects. Prune shrubs regularly to maintain compact growth.

Other host plants to aid biological pest control include brassicas, which are left to flower, parsnip, carrots, parsley, angelica, fennel, thyme and coriander.

Also attractive to predatory beneficial insects are alliums, borage, bergamot, mints, spearmint, *Digitalis ferruginea*, yarrow, artemisias, cosmos, michaelmas daisies and other daisy species. Purple-flowered *Verbena bonariensis* is an essential food station for bees, hoverflies, butterflies and moths. Add lavenders and as much phacelia as you can cram in, and you've an instant bee garden!

Healthy new season's vegetables emerge from well-composted raised beds and young seedlings are warmed and protected from the birds with a mesh frame. Plantings of chives and calendula help to repel chewing pests and borders of lobelia flowers attract bees and beneficial insects.

manure crop such as blue-flowered lupins or phacelia while not in use, than bare and weed-infested. Quick-growing, green manure plants have strong roots which help break up the soil; some add nitrogen, or draw out minerals, which are then available to following crops; some, such as rye, cleanse the soil. Cut down and allowed to dry, green manures produce a thick mass of beneficial mulch or compost.

Green manure plants

Mustard

Common mustard is hardy, grows fast as a filler or cover plant (three weeks), and if allowed to grow-on, has bright green foliage and yellow or white flowers. Cut or dug in, it decomposes quickly. Mustard is beneficial as an underplanting for tomatoes and is said to disinfect the soil, but in this position it must be trimmed back to about 30 cm (1 ft) high.

Lupins

The ordinary, quick-to-mature, blue-flowered variety is the most beneficial.

Phacelia

In addition to its role as a feeding and breeding station for beneficial insects, phacelia is an excellent green manure. There are two popular varieties, *P. tanacetifolia* and *P. campanularia*, the former has soft violet-blue feathery flowers, and the latter dark blue bells. Phacelia also enriches the soil with nitrogen, and is both a quick filler and a beautiful flowering plant which blooms over a long season.

Making compost

Well-rotted, bulky organic matter or compost is the very basis of fertility in the garden. A soil conditioner second to none, it is high in nutritional properties, improves both drainage and moisture-retaining capacity, and provides a home for millions of beneficial micro-organisms.

The most popular method of composting is known as the aerobic method, which produces usable compost in around three months. You'll require a robust bin such as the black polythene composters stocked by garden centres. They're bottomless and have ventilation holes in their sides and a lid on top. Their one disadvantage is that it can be difficult to fork and turn the compost while it is maturing. When the material is ready for use, the entire shell of the bin is lifted up, leaving a neat cone-shaped pile.

Alternatively you can construct a compost container of wooden slats, bricks or netting, which allows air to circulate but is enclosed enough to encourage heat to build up within the organic materials. If possible, it's best to build two bins side by side, so that by the time the second bin is full

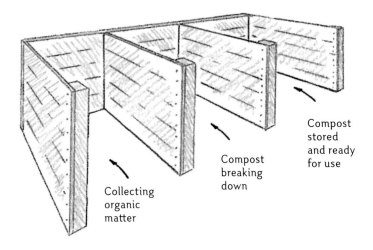

3-bay composting system

Compost stored and ready for use

Compost breaking down

Collecting organic matter

Corrugated iron and wooden stakes

Wooden bin

A small compost bin that can be turned

Whether constructed of wood, corrugated iron, polythene, bricks or netting, bin construction should allow air to circulate. It is best to build two or three bins side by side. By the time the second bin is full, the compost in the first bin should be ready for use.

the compost in the first should be ready for use. This way one always has some of this organic staff-of-life compost to hand.

To start making your compost, pierce the soil beneath where you are going to place the bin with a fork to allow excess water to drain away and encourage earthworms to rise and start work on the organic matter. Mix the materials to be composted well and place in the container in layers about 30 cm (1 ft) thick with a sprinkling of activator between layers. This can be a proprietary product, ammonium sulphate or animal manure.

When the bin is full, cover and leave it to heat up. The heating process, which takes about a month, ensures that the seeds of weeds and any pathogens are destroyed. At this stage the compost should be turned and re-covered. The process will need repeating once more before the compost is properly mature — the finest, crumbliest, sweetest-smelling soil conditioner imaginable!

Watering

No matter how well you mulch or compost, the vegetable garden has to be watered. Home-grown produce, although healthy and organically grown, won't be cost-effective if you spend hours hand-watering. Garden centres offer a wide range of relatively inexpensive DIY irrigation and sprinkler systems which will efficiently water all parts of the edible garden when required.

As worms eat their way through the vegetative waste in the worm farm trays they leave behind rich castings called vermicast, a highly nutritious fertiliser for addition to soil and compost, and to seeding or pottimg mix mediums.

Below: Overlaying well-composted vegetable beds, a top dressing of pea straw seals in soil moisture and inhibits weed growth.

Domestic worm farms

Requiring little space, inexpensive commercially produced worm farm units usually consist of four trays stacked one on top of the other. They work on the principle that as the worms eat their way up through the food in the trays, they leave behind their processed food as rich black castings called vermicast. The feeder trays may be filled with organic vegetative and kitchen waste. Avoid adding cooked food as this causes the fertiliser to smell unpleasant and may attract vermin. The bottom collector tray has a solid base and tap. Liquid seepage also drains down through the upper trays into the collector tray. To make a rich liquid fertiliser, drain off the seepage and mix with water on a 50:50 basis.

Composting worms are different to soil-dwelling earthworms. Called 'tigers' and 'reds' because of their reddish-striped bodies, they live, breed and feed under organic vegetative litter. Although the producers of commercially made units recommend the use of tiger worms, one can make a perfectly efficient domestic worm farm using the common soil-dwelling earthworm. Vermicast is nature's supreme fertiliser and improves the colour, quantity and quality of both edible and ornamental plants. It may be used as a pure organic fertiliser or as an additive to compost, seed-raising mix or potting mix.

- Seed raising mix: Three parts compost to one part vermicast.
- Potting mix: Two parts aged compost to one part vermicast.
- Top dressing: Spread a layer of vermicast 12 mm (1/2 in) deep around plants. Water in well.

You can also make your own worm farm by building a series of simple interlocking and stacking trays from untreated wood. The chemicals in treated timber will kill worms. Worm farms and worms are available from most nurseries stocking garden supplies.

Mulches

Mulches are invaluable for inhibiting weed growth, helping to retain moisture in the soil by preventing evaporation and, if they contain plenty of organic materials, they'll also feed and condition the soil thereby helping to produce bumper crops. However, gardeners have divided opinions about mulch in the ornamental edible garden where aesthetics are of importance.

It is true that any mulch which doesn't consist of equal-sized pieces looks messy, and layers of pea straw are scratched up by the birds and blow about. Mulches of bark are not suitable for the edible garden — which takes us right back to the excellent organic mulch from the compost bin!

Try to have a light layer of compost and well-rotted manure covering the soil at all times. This feeds the plants and keeps roots moist. Mulches of green manure crops grown as part of the crop rotation plan are excellent —

cut down and spread on top of the soil or dug in, they feed and protect the soil. (See Green Manures, page 131.)

Pest & disease control

As we've seen, the purpose of organic gardening is to control pests and diseases without the use of toxic pesticides and fungicides, and to maintain a conditioned, nutrient-rich soil free from chemical fertilisers.

Organic pesticides & fungicides

Nurseries offer a good range of organic sprays made from plant derivatives such as garlic, chilli, pyrethrum, rotenone and Neemseed oil, and others manufactured from non-toxic oils, soaps and fatty acids. It is possible to make your own sprays but their shelf life is limited and constantly making small amounts is time-consuming. A 200 ml bottle of commercially prepared concentrate will provide enough spray for a year or more in a medium-sized garden, and have an extended shelf life.

Remember that organic sprays, with the exception of Neemseed oil, are non-systemic — they kill or repel by actual contact with the insect pests, so all parts of the plant, including the underside of the leaves, must be thoroughly covered.

It is essential that organic sprays are used at the recommended strengths. It's tempting to make them stronger where severe infestations of pests and diseases exist, but it's more important to remember that, used in excess, they can be as lethal as non-organic preparations to insects both good and bad — and to the very plants we're trying to protect!

Sprays derived from plants
Pesticides & anti-feedants

Plant-derived sprays fall into two categories: pesticides and anti-feedants. The pesticides kill the pest while the anti-feedants repel so that the pest doesn't settle on the plant and feed from it.

Derris dust (Rotenone)

Derived from the roots of a South African tree, *Derris elliptica*, and ground into a fine powder. Derris dust kills cabbage white butterflies, beetles and other sap-sucking and chewing insects.

Dipel (Bacillus thuringiensis)

A bacterial form of biological control made from the soil bacterium *Bacillus thuringiensis*, which produces a natural toxin known as 'Bt'. Though harmless to people, animals and beneficial insects, it kills caterpillars, beetles and other sap-sucking insects. Dipel is usually available as a fine, white powder and is applied as a spray.

Neemseed oil insecticide

Oil from the neem tree (*Azadirachta indica*) is the only broad-spectrum plant-derived systemic organic pesticide currently available. It kills plant-feeding and sucking pests such as aphids, whitefly, scale, mealy bugs, caterpillars, thrips and nematodes. Neemseed oil also suppresses appetite, affects bowel activity and disrupts the development of the pests' eggs, larvae and pupae. Azadirachtin, the main ingredient of neemseed oil, is harmless to beneficial insects and predators.

Neemseed oil has been used for centuries in India as a food preservative and to prevent insects eating stored grain. Available from most nurseries.

An effective home-made pesticticide spray may be made with a cake of neem soap from a Trade Aid shop. You'll need a grater, a cake of neem soap, a 5-litre (10-pint) bucket, a whisk and a sieve, storage jars or bottles (and a strong arm). Grate a quarter of a cake of neem into bucket, pour on 1 litre (2 pints) of boiling water to make a liquid, stir thoroughly to dissolve lumps, then add 4 more litres (8 pints) of water. Strain liquid into bottles or jars. Label clearly and store in a cool place.

Fatty acids
Marketed under various names such as Naturasoap, these pesticides are manufactured from biodegradable fatty acids, natural soaps and vegetable/coconut oils in the form of a soluble concentrate. The preparation kills aphids, greenfly, mealy bugs, mites, thrips and whitefly.

Garlic & pyrethrum
Concentrated extracts of garlic, pyrethrum and sometimes chilli, freely available from garden centres, are commonly combined to create a broad-spectrum spray.

The garlic repels pests and the chilli and pyrethrum kill those that persist. Pyrethrum comes from *Chrysanthemum cinerariifolium*, commonly known as the silver-leafed pyrethrum daisy, which contains substances called pyrethrins that kill aphids, thrips, mites and caterpillars. They also kill bees and other beneficial insects, so spray only after sundown when the good guys have finished working the flowers.

Garlic spray (repellent)
To make your own garlic spray, chop 6 large cloves of garlic and place in a blender with 6 tablespoons of medicinal paraffin oil and pulverise. Leave pulp to stand for 48 hours.

Grate 1 tablespoon of oil-based soap into a container and add 500 ml (1 pint) of hot water, stirring until the soap has melted. Stir into the garlic pulp. When cool, strain into jars, label clearly and store in the refrigerator. When spraying, use 2 tablespoons garlic mixture to 1 litre (2 pints) of water.

Pyrethrum insecticide
Take 1 tablespoon of well-crushed flowers of the silver-leafed pyrethrum daisy, *Chrysanthemum cinerariifolium* (syn. *Pyrethrum cinerariifolium*), and mix with sufficient spirit alcohol to wet the flowers and release the pyrethrin extracts. (Flowers may be harvested, dried and stored for use at other times of the year.) Place the crushed mixture into 2 litres (4 pints) of hot water and add a squirt of soft or natural soap (not detergent) to aid stickability. Stand and strain into airtight jars when cool. Label clearly and store in the refrigerator.

Three-in-one repellent, pesticide & fungicide spray
Garlic, pyrethrum and copper oxychloride (see below) preparations are all compatible and when combined in the exact dilutions recommended by the manufacturer, create a spray that protects edible and ornamental plants against pests, and fungal and bacterial diseases. Garlic acts as an insect-repellent, pyrethrum as an organic insecticide and copper oxychloride as a protection against fungal and bacterial diseases.

Fungicides
Copper oxychloride fungicides

Copper oxychloride fungicides ('Super Copper DF' (('Kocide df')) active ingredient 400 kg/copper as cupric hydroxide) are manufactured in the form of a wettable powder which controls fungal and bacterial diseases, such as blight, downy mildew, black spot, leaf curl and shothole. (Shothole is a disease affecting stone fruit. It causes brown patches on the leaves, which then dry out leaving a hole on the leaf.)

Although an effective fungicide, copper oxychloride solution washes off in the lightest shower. It will give continued protection if mixed into a carrying base.

To prepare a base, combine 2.5 tablespoons of a mineral oil with 4.5 litres (8.5 pints) of water. Add 1 tablespoon of soft liquid soap, which will help the spray adhere to foliage. Mix the copper oxychloride solution according to the manufacturer's dilution rate, add to the base and apply.

Dozing on duty, the sleepy scarecrow needs the help of benign sprays and companion plants to protect organically grown crops. Blue-flowered *Phacelia tanacetifolia* (front left) is an important host plant for beneficial insects that prey on insect pests. Borders of chives around the old pink rose act as repellent plants. Intensive vegetable production in a small area such as this is also helped by well-conditioned and humus-enriched soil.

Slug & snail deterrents
Barrier control

Slug and snail pellets used to contain concentrated chemicals which were toxic to children, pets, hedgehogs and birds, however low-toxicity pellets are now available. They contain iron chelate, which slows the pest's metabolism down until death occurs.

For added safety, conceal the pellets in short lengths of plastic piping beneath plants. This will also keep them dry. Slug and snail pellets need renewing after rain.

Other non-toxic products to deter slugs and snails are composed mainly of coarse, gritty powders which work on a barrier principle — like crushed eggshells. The jaws of the gastropod world will not cross sharp or gritty substances, so ringing plants with these materials gives protection.

The preparations need to be applied regularly, particularly after rain. Clear-plastic bottles with the bottoms cut out also form excellent protection and insulation for young plants.

A walk around the garden after dark with torch and stout boots is also a good form of gastropod despatch!

Fungicide for black spot & downy mildew

Take 1 teaspoon of baking soda, 1 teaspoon of Codacide oil (a vegetable oil) and mix with 1 litre (2 pints) of water. Spray every 10 days for continued protection against black spot and mildew. Particularly effective on roses and cucurbits.

Conqueror spraying oil, pest oil, Codacide, all-purpose oil & mineral oil

These non-toxic mineral or vegetable oils control downy mildew and fungal diseases, scale, mites, leaf miner and and mealy bugs on citrus, fruit and vegetables.

They are compatible with copper oxychloride fungicide preparations and can be used together as an organic pesticide and fungicide. The combination is efficient as a general clean-up spray before and after pruning and during winter. The oils are for use in both winter and early summer.

When home-made pesticides are cool and strained, bottle, label clearly and store in a cool, dark place.

Barriers & other organic plant protection methods

Trees, particularly fruiting varieties, can be protected against flightless insects by having sticky bands and collars placed around the base of the trunk. These trap the larvae as they crawl up the trunk from the ground. The band should be thickly coated with Vaseline, engine grease or any other sticky non-toxic material.

To protect fruit trees from codling moth, use commercially made traps which emit female hormonal scents (pheromones). These attract male moths and when they have entered the trap, they are trapped by the sticky material at the base.

The traps should be used when the moths start flying in spring. Sticky band collars will also trap codling moth caterpillars as they descend the tree in late summer. Check bands regularly for live pests and destroy.

A product recently on the market is a type of glue gun containing a sticky, long-lasting barrier preparation. Applied as a ring around the trunk, this traps undesirable insects trying to move either up or down the tree.

Pests and diseases on trees are also controlled by frequent applications of the organic sprays already discussed, used at slightly stronger concentration. Copper and mineral oil preparations are particularly good for the prevention and treatment of brown rot and leaf curl on peach, plum and nectarine trees, and for fungal diseases.

Quick-reference guide to preventing plague & pestilence

● **PESTS**

Aphids, greenfly, whitefly, mealy bugs, mites, thrips and leaf miner
Treatment: Naturasoap and other fatty acid/oil-based sprays; soapy water; pyrethrum; pest and mineral oils; garlic concentrate; Neemseed oil. Mealy bug infestations can be treated by brushing with a 50:50 mix of methylated spirits and water.

Caterpillars, leaf-rollers
Treatment: Derris dust; Neemseed oil; Dipel.

Scale
Treatment: Scrub off with nailbrush or toothbrush dipped in a weak solution of water, oil and vinegar.

Beetles: green and bronze
Treatment: Dipel; Neemseed oil; fish emulsion and garlic sprays (repellents). Remove manually.

Slugs and snails
Treatment: Low-toxicity bait pellets and coarse preparations containing gritty, sandy substances. Spraying with wormwood infusion (see page 135).

● **FUNGAL DISEASES**

Blight, powdery mildew, downy mildew, damping-off disease of seedlings, rust
Treatment: Regular spraying with mineral oil concentrates and copper hydroxic-based fungicide sprays.

The organic edible garden

The purpose of organic gardening is to strengthen the plant's resistance to diseases and pests without resorting to unnatural agencies. The soil is a living organism and remains healthy if it is used and fertilised biologically. Consider the thought that 'bios' is Greek for life; biology is the science of life; biological means are those according to the laws of life.

Healthy soil = healthy plants = healthy people!

Accept that, initially, going organic takes courage and a few dark nights of the soul, when the whole garden seems to be chewed, razored, pock-marked or reduced to a skeleton. Be assured that your garden, and the birds and the bees that share it, will ultimately thrive as beneficial insects and pestiferous ones find a natural balance.

Screw up your courage, go forth and plant your edible garden for the new season, and throw out those prettily packaged poisons!

Even one lonely snail can do significant damage to a treasured crop, and just wait to see what can happen when the rest of the family arrives! It pays to be vigilant with these pesky pests.

Bibliography

Art of French Vegetable Gardening, Louisa Jones, Artisan Publishing, 1995.

Kings Seed Catalogue Australia & New Zealand 1996/97, Kings Herb, 1996

The Complete New Zealand Gardener, Geoff Bryant & Eion Scarrow, David Bateman Ltd, 1995

The Herb Garden Displayed, Gilian Painter & Elaine Power, Hodder & Stoughton, 1979

The Ornamental Kitchen Garden, Janet MacDonald, David & Charles, 1994 (Extract used by kind permission of the publishers.)

The Traditional Rose Garden, Graham Rose, Dorling Kindersley, 1989

Acknowledgements

My heartfelt thanks to my editor, Caroline List, for the time, skill and patience she put into shaping and producing this book.

The author, photographer and publisher would like to thank:

Annabel Langbein, pp. 53, 61 (top & bottom), 65, 70 (bottom), 74 (top), 101 (bottom), 102, 134 (bottom)

Anne Norris, p. 23

Annie Heywood, p. 113

Auckland Botanical Gardens, pp. 54, 56 (top), 70 (top), 72 (top), 80, 126, 128

Barewood, Caroline & Joe Ferraby pp. 6, 22, 24, 32, 43 (left), 45, 84 (top & bottom), 94

Barnsley House, Rosemary Verey, Circencester, Gloucestershire, front cover (bottom), pp. 16 (bottom), 29 (left), 37 (bottom), 42, 48, 106 (right), 118

Bellevue, Vivian Papich, p. 111 (left)

Bourton House, Bourton-on-Mill, Gloucestershire, pp. 11 (left), 34, 40, 73 (bottom)

Christine & Philip Crawshaw, p. 28 (left)

Clare & Alex Scott, p. 29 (bottom)

Denmans, John Brookes, pp. 1, 100

Gethsemane, Bev & Ken Loader, p. 27 (bottom)

Julia & Andrew Everist, pp. 49, 99

Julie Fulton, p. 14

Kay Green, pp. 12, 13 (bottom)

Kelmano Gardens, p. 92

Kiri Kiri Gardens, Robyn & Joe Woollaston, p. 28 (right)

Koanga Nurseries, p. 107

Le Potager, Joanna Stewart, pp. 15, 71, 96

Liz Caughey, p. 127

Liz Mackmurdie, pp. 10, 36 (top), 44, 106 (left), 108, 130 (top)

Moss Green Gardens, Jo & Bob Munro, pp. 36 (bottom), 132

Nancy McCabe, Falls Village, Connecticut, pp. 35 (right), 110 (top & bottom)

Nymet, Jean & Colin Sanders, p. 35 (left)

Ohinetahi, Sir Miles Warren, p. 52

Olive Dunn, back cover, p. 46

Penny Wiggin, pp. 86, 88

Peter Worsp, Terra Viva Nursery, Christchurch, pp. 47, 98, 116, 119

Phil Cooke, pp. 16 (top), 17, 117

Philip Stray & Philip Johnson, Melbourne, pp. 8, 26

Rathmoy, Suzanne Grace, p. 33

Richard Luisetti, p. 101 (top)

Rob Watson, Christchurch, p. 115

Robyn Sygrove, p. 111 (right)

Rodney Fumpston, pp. 43 (right), 105

Rosemoor Gardens, Great Torrington, Devon, pp. 31, 103

Shackleton Gardens, Clonsilla, Dublin, p. 50

Sue Paluvinskas, Coatesville, pp. 3, 41, 56 (bottom), 58 (bottom), 93

The Master's Garden, Lord Leycester Hospital, Warwickshire, pp. 27 (top), 30 (top), 37 (top), 76

The Milton Vineyard, p. 38

The Old Rectory, Mr & Mrs Anthony Huntington, Sudsborough, Kettering, pp. 4, 39, 82

Valley Homestead, Diana & Brian Anthony, pp. 13 (top), 120, 137

Winterholme, Susan & Richard McFarlane, Kaikoura, front cover (top), pp. 9, 87

Woodbridge, Christine & Tony Peak, Coatesville, pp. 30 (bottom), 63 (bottom), 67, 74 (bottom), 78 (bottom), 81

Index

Entries in *italics* denote references to photographs and tables